HISTORY OF
THE UNITED STATES

VOLUME VII

THE KENNEDY YEARS

THE MARCH
OF DEMOCRACY

A HISTORY OF THE UNITED STATES

By James Truslow Adams

Continued by Jacob E. Cooke

Professor of History, Lafayette College

Volume VII

THE KENNEDY YEARS

CHARLES SCRIBNER'S SONS
NEW YORK

PREFACE

JOHN F. KENNEDY was a worthy successor to such patrician reformers as Thomas Jefferson and Franklin D. Roosevelt. His presidency, unfortunately, was too brief for him to leave as great an impact on our day as his great Democratic predecessors left on theirs. Nevertheless, the years 1960-63 will, for the calculable future, be associated with his name.

When Kennedy was elected President on November 8, 1960, many Americans were troubled by his youth and inexperience. He had, to be sure, ably served as senator from Massachusetts since 1952, but his administrative experience was unimpressive, his ability to handle the complexities of foreign affairs undemonstrated, and his willingness to exercise the bold leadership necessary to arouse the nation to the need for new and imaginative solutions to domestic difficulties untested.

During his years as President, Kennedy removed such doubts. He proved himself to be a forceful executive, in the tradition of Woodrow Wilson and the two Roosevelts. After a bad bungle at the Bay of Pigs invasion in April, 1961, he handled the country's foreign problems with admirable adroitness and patience. From the day of his inauguration until his death in Dallas, Texas, some 33 months later, he constantly challenged the American people and their representatives in Congress to solve the problems of a sluggish economy and technological unemployment, of racial discrimination in schools, voting and jobs, of deteriorating cities and regional poverty, and of inadequate medical care for the aged and inadequate education for the young.

v

2481

Only a part of the Kennedy program was enacted into law. Whether or not more of it would have been had the President lived and been elected to a second term is, obviously, futile speculation. That it was not is attributable less to the quality of his leadership than to the opposition he encountered—the hostility of die-hard segregationists in the South, the unwillingness of Congress to share his vision of the future, and the popular complacency engendered by prosperity. Yet, his accomplishments at home and abroad, as the following chapters abundantly attest, were impressive. If it is too early to tell whether Kennedy, despite the short time he held the office, was a great President, it is at least certain that he was an extraordinarily capable one.

JACOB E. COOKE

CONTENTS

ILLUSTRATIONS

IN TEXT

On January 20, 1961, John Fitzgerald Kennedy was inaugurated 35th President of the United States.

"Let the word go forth from this time and place, to friend and foe alike, that the torch has passed to a new generation of Americans—born in this century, tempered by war, disciplined by a hard and bitter peace, proud of our ancient heritage. . . ."

As Kennedy, the youngest President ever to assume office in the United States, delivered these ringing inaugural phrases in a flat New England accent which seemed strangely inappropriate to their eloquence, Dwight D. Eisenhower, the oldest man ever to occupy the White House, sat on the flag-decked platform, his face registering no emotion except that of concentration. He might well have been asking himself whether youth, energy, and determination were enough to overcome the ineluctable problems he had sought to resolve for eight years.

The problems confronting the new President were, indeed, formidable; perhaps they were problems for which no solution could be found. When Franklin

Delano Roosevelt became President in 1933, he was confronted by a sagging economy, millions of unemployed, a loss of confidence in government. Yet these were problems about which something could be done; action on them was at least not dependent on the notorious vagaries of international politics. For Kennedy, the situation was different. Domestic problems were overshadowed by and intertwined with international concerns of far greater magnitude.

The difficulties which faced Kennedy were, in effect, the same difficulties which had faced Truman in 1949 and Eisenhower in 1953. How could the United States maintain the highest living standard in the world while appropriating ever larger amounts of money for an increasingly complex and expensive military organization? What measures could the United States adopt to bolster the free world against the threat of international communism? In what way and to what extent should we help the underdeveloped nations of the world? What type of defense was best for a country faced both with the possibility of nuclear war and the threat of limited-scope wars calling for conventional weapons? Finally, how best could the United States help to preserve the peace of the world—by relying solely on its military might or by negotiating with the Russians?

In his inaugural address President Kennedy exuded confidence, but he did not promise easy solutions to these persistent problems. Instead he called on the

American people to meet these challenges with vigor and with a freshness of approach. "All this will not be finished in the first 100 days," he said. "Nor will it be finished in the first 1,000 days, nor in the life of this Administration, nor even perhaps in our lifetime on this planet. But let us begin." The poet Robert Frost heralded Kennedy's administration as "an Augustan age of poetry and power, with the emphasis on power."

To be rightly understood, President Kennedy's conduct of foreign policy must be viewed in the context of the world-wide struggle against international communism which the United States has waged since World War II. Had this perspective been kept in mind, many of the President's supporters—chiefly liberal intellectuals —would have been spared considerable disappointment. Among those who argued that American foreign policy under Eisenhower had been stagnant and sterile, it was widely believed that Kennedy quickly would solve many of the problems that have trammeled our relations with Russia for a decade and a half. Such a view was naive, and the President was culpable only to the extent that he encouraged it. During his campaign for the presidency, Kennedy had lent support to these great expectations; by criticizing the unimaginativeness and inertia of Eisenhower's foreign policy, he implied that if elected he would be able considerably to improve our international posture. But President Kennedy, and with him many of his most ardent supporters, was soon taught the lesson which President Eisenhower had learned long since—that the shrewdness of the leaders in the Kremlin as much determines American policy as the intelligence of planners in the State Department; that inertia is often preferable to precipitate and unwise action; and that new policies are limited by the attitudes of our allies as well as the sensibilities of the uncommitted nations.

The most direct Soviet imperialist threat in the year 1961 was in Berlin, but the Communist challenge was truly global. It had to be met in Asia, where Communist aggression threatened the independence of Laos and South Vietnam; in Africa, where the Communists sought a close alliance with new nations like the Congo; and in Latin America, where Cuba, close to the shores of the United States, had allied itself with the Communist bloc.

When Kennedy first took office there was excited speculation that he would inaugurate creative and important changes in American foreign policy. In Laos he seemed moving toward an acceptance of the solution which Eisenhower never quite accepted—the creation of an all-embracing government of national unity under the premiership of Prince Souvanna Phouma. It was not entirely out of the question that Kennedy might use the good will which a new President customarily enjoys to offer "some kind" of recognition to the Communist government in China. It also was hinted that the Administration might persuade its Western allies to recognize the Communist East German regime if the Russians, in return, would guarantee the West's right of access to Berlin. On the vitally important question of disarmament, the new President early made it clear that he would accept a treaty banning nuclear tests (subject to agreement on a reasonably adequate control system) rather than take advantage of the military benefits of continued testing. Yet by the end of the year Kennedy's initial attempts to take bold strides in settling our international problems had been thwarted. Were the road blocks which he encountered thrown up by Khrushchev and Castro, by de Gaulle and Adenauer, by Congress and his domestic opponents, or, perhaps, by his own ineptitude and inexperience? The answer is to be found in a closer examination of American foreign policy during the year.

Immediately before and for a short time after Kennedy's inauguration Premier Nikita Khrushchev chose to display the genial and cooperative side of his many-faceted personality. On the day of his inauguration, for example, Kennedy received a telegram from the Russian Premier which read: "Dear Mr. President, we congratulate you upon your inauguration. We avail ourselves of the opportunity to express the hope that . . . we shall . . . attain a radical improvement of relations between our countries. . . ." In a characteristically dramatic gesture, Khrushchev next released two American fliers whose imprisonment as "spies" had intensified international rancor during the closing months of the

Eisenhower era. Kennedy replied by promising not to send any more reconnaissance flights over Russia, thus demonstrating American good will and at the same time depriving Khrushchev of the issue which he had used to such good advantage in breaking up the Paris summit conference in June, 1960. A few intrepid optimists immediately proclaimed the inauguration of a new era of Soviet-American relations, but even before the new Administration had time seriously to weigh the sincerity of Mr. Khrushchev's peaceful pronouncements, the Russian Premier resumed his more characteristic bellicose stance.

The chief issue of Kennedy's first three months in office, however, was the specific threat of Communist inroads in Laos and Cuba. Cuba and Laos demonstrated how difficult it is to change the direction of the ship of state, especially if it has been traveling the same course for more than a decade; they symbolized, furthermore, the frustration of the American attempt to impose its standards on these areas.

The most serious mistake which President Kennedy made in the year 1961 was his decision to sanction the invasion of Cuba. The invasion was perhaps the logical conclusion to the Cuban policy pursued by the Eisenhower Administration during 1960, a policy which had culminated in Eisenhower's decision in January, 1961, to break off relations with Cuba. But however difficult it might have been to reverse the policies of his predecessor, Kennedy was assuredly responsible for one of the worst foreign policy blunders in recent history.

The Cuban invasion was carried out by anti-Castro exiles known as the *Frente* (Democratic Revolutionary Front) which had begun recruiting volunteers in New York and Florida for a projected invasion as early as the spring of 1960. Military preparations were well advanced by the time Kennedy took office. That the new President did not cancel them was owing chiefly to the intelligence reports submitted to him by the Central Intelligence Agency and approved by the Pentagon; the landing of the exiles, these reports stated, would immediately produce a popular uprising in Cuba which Castro's forces would not be able to quell. The policy which Kennedy followed was also due to his own highly emotional reaction to the Castro regime, a reaction that had been evident in his speeches during the presidential campaign.

Just before dawn on April 17 some 1,200 anti-Castro troops were put ashore at Bahia de Cochinos (Bay of Pigs), on the southern coast of central Cuba. For three days the fate of the invaders was unknown; Castro had imposed a total communications blackout, and there were no newsmen with the rebel forces. Then, the bleak truth began to be known. No mass uprisings had occurred in the island. Not a single radio transmitter had been secured for broadcasting news of the invasion among the allegedly oppressed Cubans. The rebel force had been decimated and routed by superior artillery, tanks and planes; after only two days, it had retreated to the beach and dispersed.

The Kennedy Administration was responsible both for the invasion and for its failure. The President had had control over the operation, for the United States provided the financial backing, the organization and the equipment which made possible the launching of the invasion. Nor was it denied that the CIA contributed to the support of the exiles in Florida by an estimated $150,000 to $400,000 a month, provided instructors in guerrilla warfare, acquired airfields no longer in use and set up training camps in Guatemala. Abroad, the prestige of the United States suffered a major blow. In the United States there was an agonized reappraisal of our Cuban policy. What kind of intelligence system, it was asked, could have supplied reports so obviously at variance with the facts?

The President did not shirk personal responsibility for the invasion but he hastened to impose the doctrine of collective responsibility on American institutions and political leaders. Salvage operations were begun immediately. A review of the operation was undertaken by the usual "task force"; Gen. Maxwell Taylor was named to handle the CIA; bipartisan backing was sought by meetings with Eisenhower, former Vice President Nixon, Sen. Barry Goldwater, Gov. Nelson Rockefeller, former President Hoover and Gen. Douglas MacArthur. Kennedy's recovery from the Cuban fiasco was a masterpiece of political dexterity.

8

Cuba was perhaps more a domestic than an international problem, for it can be argued that the Cuban invasion was in large part a reflection of a popular view that what happens in Cuba is our especial business. Events in the kingdom of Laos, however, for some time the chief trouble spot in southeast Asia, were a clear-cut case of Communist aggression. At the beginning of the year 1961, the pro-Western Laotian regime of Premier Boun Oum, supplied with arms by the United States, was locked in battle with an alliance of the Communist Pathet Lao and neutralist forces equipped by the Soviets. There was increasing anxiety that Laos might become another Korea.

When President Kennedy took office he was confronted by a difficult dilemma. Should he try to prevent the Communist conquest of all Laos by stepping up American aid to pro-Western forces, or should he rely on the slender reed of Russian good faith and agree to submit the question to negotiation? An expensive and unsuccessful war would probably soon become unpopular in the United States; the Republican cry that the Democrats get the country into wars would soon drown the initial show of Republican support in Congress. On the other hand, the loss of another country behind the iron curtain would provide the opposition with new ammunition. Determined not to be trapped by this dilemma, the President sought to resolve it by announcing that the United States wanted a "neutral and independent" Laos not dominated by either side.

9

The Russians, however, showed little interest in proposals by the United States for a neutralist Laos. Moscow stepped up its aid to the Pathet Lao and by mid-March appeared to be engaged in a major military offensive. On March 19, Kennedy retaliated by announcing that aid to Boun Oum had been increased and that additional technicians to help train the Laotian army had been sent. Only two months after taking office President Kennedy found himself faced with risks in Laos similar to those which President Truman had faced in Korea more than ten years before.

Fortunately, Premier Khrushchev was not as willing to risk war as Stalin and Mao Tse-tung had been in 1950; the Russian Premier was apparently persuaded that he could gain his objectives as easily by diplomatic duplicity. Early in April, therefore, the Soviet Union agreed in principle to a Western proposal for a cease-fire to be followed by an international conference.

On May 12 fourteen nations assembled in Geneva to try to resolve the Laotian issue. The participating nations were the "Big Four," China, the four Indo-Chinese states, Thailand and Burma (neighbors of Laos), and India, Canada, and Poland (the three members of the International Control Commission which was established for Laos in 1954, dissolved in 1958, and renewed in April, 1961, to police the cease-fire agreed on by the Big Powers). During the first few weeks of the conference very little was accomplished. The Western delegates supported a plan which would give the International Control Commission additional powers and allow it to operate under majority rule; the Soviet bloc and China insisted that the Commission must not "interfere in the domestic affairs" of Laos and demanded that decisions of the Commission be unanimous, thus giving Communist Poland a veto. There was also disagreement on the composition of any future Laotian government. The seriousness of these disagreements, however, was mitigated by the possibility of agreement between Kennedy and Khrushchev at the approaching Vienna summit meeting.

The turn of events in Cuba and also in Laos forced the Kennedy Administration to take a new look at its opposition to summit conferences with Mr. Khrushchev. Before he took office the President had insisted that personal talks with the Soviet leader would be postponed until visible progress had been made towards better relations with Russia through normal diplomatic methods. Now, only a little more than four months after his inauguration, Kennedy decided to meet Khrushchev face to face. The President's decision was not altogether a free one. For one thing, repeated setbacks in foreign affairs made a personal meeting with Mr. Khrushchev appear an attractive way of ascertaining what, and to what extent, East-West differences were negotiable. For another, the announcement that Kennedy would visit President de Gaulle early in June gave Khrushchev a perfect opening to suggest that the President's presence in Europe provided a convenient opportunity for a meeting. To have refused such an invitation might well have made it appear that Kennedy was opposed to negotiation.

Early in April, the President had embarked upon talks with America's allies in order to define common objectives for dealing with the Communist challenge. He met first in the nation's capital with British Prime Minister Harold Macmillan; then, also in Washington, with West German Chancellor Adenauer. To work out a common policy with Macmillan and Adenauer was comparatively easy; to reach an understanding with President Charles de Gaulle of France was a job to test the patience and skill of the most able diplomat. De Gaulle's demands for a three-power directorate of the Western alliance by the United States, Britain, and France; his opposition to integration of French military forces in NATO; his insistence on developing an independent nuclear deterrent; his hostility toward the UN; his steadfast opposition to negotiation with the Russians over Berlin; all these things indicated how difficult it would be to secure his cooperation in any common policy devised by the other Western nations.

President Kennedy's three-day stay in Paris was a great personal success. It was even more a personal success for Mrs. Kennedy whose good looks, charm, ability to speak French and obvious enthusiasm for French culture won her the type of acclaim which is usually reserved for screen stars or royalty. The diplomatic success of the meeting was less certain. Kennedy and de Gaulle held frequent conferences, after which it was announced that the two leaders had identical views on their commitments and responsibilities in Berlin and were in "fundamental agreement" on a broad range of problems. The sanguine tone of the communique deceived no one, however. Kennedy may have charmed de Gaulle but he had not altered the General's policies.

On June 3 Kennedy flew to Vienna for his crucial encounter with Khrushchev. The meeting was brief and the notice of it so short that the press was unable to build up exaggerated hopes about its outcome. The extremes of press hysteria which made the meeting at Geneva in 1955 seem like the beginning of a new world and the conference in Paris in 1960 like the imminent end of the old one were thus avoided. Khrushchev handed Kennedy an *aide-mémoire* which declared that Russia "deems it necessary to normalize the situation in West Berlin" and spoke of six months as the deadline for a solution. Failing agreement, he warned, Russia would sign a separate peace treaty with East Germany—which would have the effect of turning over to the East German regime the control of Western military access routes to Berlin. Khrushchev also insisted on the *troika* system for giving the Russians a veto on enforcement of the ban on atomic tests. Finally, he revealed clearly his confidence that the West would cave in, that the Russians were at the controls of the locomotive of history, the course of which the United States could do nothing to divert. The only positive accomplishment of the talks was an agreement in principle on the neutrality of Laos.

In the weeks following the Vienna conference international tension mounted alarmingly. Khrushchev continued to threaten that he would sign a separate peace treaty with the East Germans "this year," insisted that the negotiations for a nuclear test ban be merged with his obviously unacceptable demand for a "general and complete disarmament," proclaimed a 33 percent increase in Russia's military budget and called off a 1,200,-000 man troop reduction previously announced. This Russian bellicosity intensified the flight of refugees from East Berlin, an exodus which was presumably a primary reason for Khrushchev's threats. Over the past years, the East Germans had used West Berlin as an escape hatch, thus draining from East Germany some 2,500,000 people, including urgently needed laborers and technicians. As fear mounted that this escape route might soon be closed, the flight developed into a stampede of more than 2,000 a day.

The fear was well-founded. At 2 A.M. on August 13 the Communists sealed off the borders between East and West Berlin. Dozens of East German tanks rumbled up to the Brandenburg Gate, the main portal between East and West Berlin and the symbol of Berlin's role as the focus of the East-West struggle. Guards pulled men and women off subway and elevated trains. A concrete barrier was erected to block off the main escape route for refugees, and barbed wire was strung across other border

'You'll Pull An Oar, Of Course?'

Charles Werner
in *The Indianapolis Star*

"Sure, I'm For Self-Determination—I Determine These Things Myself"

Herblock
in *The Washington Post*

points. East and West faced each other over the Berlin barricades with drawn guns.

Khrushchev now decided to open a new and tragic chapter in the arms race. On September 1 the Soviet Union set off a nuclear explosion over central Asia. The news sent tremors of fear through the world, for it obviously marked the failure of man's efforts to control the tremendous force that was born in the ruins of Hiroshima. Why was Khrushchev courting the risk of alienating the neutral nations which he had been wooing for so many years? Apparently he meant to emphasize that the alternative to his demands over Berlin and elsewhere might well be nuclear holocaust. The Soviet announcement had been made on the eve of a meeting in Belgrade of the twenty-five leading neutral nations; the West confidently expected that the leaders of the uncommitted nations would roundly denounce the Soviet Union. Mr. Khrushchev was obviously a shrewder judge of neutral sentiments. The conference adopted a declaration, the import of which was that the West should placate Mr. Khrushchev in order to avoid war. The declaration did not condemn the Russians for resuming tests; it merely recommended that an agreement on test suspension should be urgently concluded.

Khrushchev demonstrated his contempt for civilization and his obvious immunity from the criticism of neutral nations by continuing nuclear tests. As explosion followed explosion, radioactive clouds drifted across the northern part of the globe, possibly endangering the health of millions. On October 21, hard on the conclusion of the 22nd Soviet party conference (at which division between Russia and Communist China was made abundantly clear), Khrushchev delivered an ominous warning to his Western foes and to his Communist opponents as well. The hydrogen bomb that Russia had detonated over the Arctic on that day was more than 3,000 times as powerful, for example, as the bomb that destroyed Hiroshima in 1945; it increased the radioactive contamination of the atmosphere by half.

Within a few weeks the level of radioactive fall-out began to decline, but the political fall-out was not diminished. On September 5 the President had announced resumption by the United States of underground testing, a type of testing that produces no air-polluting fall-out. Whether or not to resume atmospheric testing was a harder question. With characteristic cunning, Khrushchev had justified his tests by insisting that they were necessary for security against "Western war preparations" over Berlin; after completing them, he called for an end to all testing. The refusal of the United States to resume tests might, on the one hand, give Russia a nuclear lead; the resumption of tests, on the other, would destroy whatever gain in world esteem our country had acquired.

Khrushchev's strategy of terror underscored the gravity of the power struggle over Berlin. Russia continued to insist on an East German peace treaty that would give her satellite regime full control of the Berlin access routes and the conversion of West Berlin into a demilitarized "free city," but by October Moscow had dropped the tough line she had assumed since the encounter at Vienna and was harping on the theme that an accommodation with the West was possible. Consistent with this new turn in Soviet diplomacy, Premier Khrushchev withdrew his threat to sign a separate peace treaty with the East Germans by the end of the year. The Western nations were still firmly committed to the ultimate reunification of Germany, to a refusal of formal recognition to the East German regime as a sovereign state, and to the principle that the West Berliners have a right to choose their own form of government and political allegiance. Khrushchev's tactical retreat, however, forced the Western allies to undertake the hard task of reconciling their own differences over what they would be willing to concede if Khrushchev agreed to a negotiated settlement.

The United States and Great Britain advocated compromise on some issues; Germany and France were vehemently opposed to any negotiations with the Russians, much less concessions. Thus the British and the Americans, while refusing to extend formal recognition to East Germany as a "sovereign" regime, were ready to deal on a *de facto* basis with the East Germans if allied rights in West Berlin could be guaranteed. West German Chancellor Conrad Adenauer endorsed the American view in December, not because he had had a change of heart, but because a truly independent foreign policy is difficult for West Germany, which is dependent on the

United States for security. This left France as the only firm holdout against negotiations.

As Premier Khrushchev once again maneuvered toward a summit meeting at which he might raise the whole spectrum of cold-war issues, the Western allies anxiously pondered his motives. Behind his beaming face, his witticisms, his displays of temper lay a mind at once Oriental and Machiavellian. Did he hope once again to divert the attention of the world from the facts of Soviet tyranny by beckoning Western leaders down the garden path of negotiation? Or did he wish sincerely to preserve the peace of the world by seeking compromises on those issues (like Berlin and disarmament) which are indeed negotiable?

The importance of the "neutral" and "underdeveloped" nations was underscored in 1961, as it had been in 1960, by the chaotic situation in the Congo. Undeniably, the Congo was a pawn in the conflict between East and West. The Communist powers, unwilling to wait for the triumph of communism in Africa which their dogma proclaims to be inevitable, worked diligently to hasten their victory. The West, concerned over Russian machinations, was unwilling passively to allow the African continent to fall to its arch rivals. To other nations, however, the Congo was chiefly a symbol of the attempt of formerly oppressed colonies to achieve statehood and an example of the impediments to freedom thrown up by the rivalry of East and West.

In the Congo the question at the beginning of the year was whether the UN Army of approximately 20,000 blue-helmeted soldiers could save the Congolese from self-destruction. There were three actors in the tragic drama being played out in the strife-torn Congo —Joseph Kasavubu, Patrice Lumumba, and Moise Tshombe. Kasavubu was the leading figure in the central government at Leopoldville. A staunch anti-Communist, he was supported by the United States and its Western allies. Patrice Lumumba, ex-premier of the Congo, was President Kasavubu's prisoner. A fiery advocate of African nationalism and an ardent foe of colonialism, Lumumba was the favorite of the Soviet bloc and of most African and Asian nations. Even in jail, his influence in the Congo seemingly remained undiminished, and Moscow confidently expected him to be released, to emerge once again as head of the government and to open the doors of the Congo to them. President Moise Tshombe of Katanga province and not Lumumba, however, was the chief stumbling block to Congo federation. Only eleven days after Congolese independence was proclaimed, the southeastern province of Katanga had seceded. Without the revenues from Katanga, whose copper mines are the richest asset of the Congo, the central government could not hope to become self-sustaining. But a settlement appeared to be impossible as long as the Belgian government and the Union Miniére, the great Belgian mining company in

20

Katanga, continued to support the secessionist movement.

No one expected a quick or easy solution to the Congo problem, but it did appear in the first weeks of 1961 that the worst of the fighting was over. Then, in mid-February, Patrice Lumumba, who had been turned over to his enemies in Katanga by the central government in Leopoldville, was brutally murdered. (A UN Commission reported later in the year that he was murdered by Katanga authorities in the presence of President Tshombe.) Unstable and unsuccessful while he was alive, Lumumba became a martyr and a symbol of pan-Africanism, anti-colonialism and anti-imperialism. His death was a blow to moderation in the Congo and was, in no sense, a success for the West. On the contrary, the angry reactions in Africa and elsewhere gave Khrushchev an opportunity to launch a fresh onslaught on the United Nations and its Secretary General, Dag Hammarskjöld. The Soviet Union immediately introduced a resolution in the United Nations Security Council calling for the resignation of Mr. Hammarskjöld, UN withdrawal from the Congo, and aid and recognition to Antoine Gizenga, the former deputy and popular heir of Lumumba.

The Western nations, unwilling to abandon the Congo to what all too clearly would be anarchy tempered by Soviet intervention, demanded a strengthened mandate for the UN force. The issue was settled by the Afro-Asians. Like the Soviets, they favored Gizenga but (unlike Premier Khrushchev) they feared that the Congo might become an arena of international conflict and that the UN would be destroyed in the process. These nations successfully sponsored a resolution which authorized "the use of force, if necessary, in the last resort," to prevent civil war in the Congo, called for the evacuation of all Belgian and other foreign military and paramilitary personnel, and recommended the reconvening of the Congolese Parliament which last had met in the summer of 1960.

Assisted by UN officials, the Congolese Parliament reconvened and on August 2 voted overwhelmingly in favor of a new prime minister, Mr. Cyrille Adoula. Despite Adoula's reputation as a socialist and a supporter of the Lumumba vision of a strong unitary form of government for the Congo, President Kasavubu, a federalist and no socialist, welcomed the new prime minister. More important, Antoine Gizenga not only recognized the new government but agreed to serve in it as first deputy premier.

The prospects for a viable Congo government were thus improved, only to be dashed by the stubbornness of Moise Tshombe, adamant foe of Congo federation. Unwilling to return Katanga to the national fold on any terms except his own, Tshombe intrenched himself in Katanga by recruiting and raising a crack force of mercenaries from Belgium, French Algeria, South Africa, and the Rhodesias. After weeks of fruitless negotiations with Tshombe, the UN took the offensive. Indian Gurkha troops were moved into Katanga, took control of the Elizabethville airport, and began an intensive search for foreign mercenaries. Tshombe resisted, and in mid-September the dispute erupted into an eight-day military conflict which was ended only when the UN, under strong pressure from Britain and France, was compelled to agree to a cease-fire. In an attempt to arrange this, Dag Hammarskjöld died in a plane crash on September 18.

As the secession continued, the authority of the Adoula government slowly disintegrated; the defiance of Katanga apparently encouraged other regions to defy the central government. Events of the rest of the year emphasized the almost insurmountable problems of the Adoula government and raised the disturbing question of whether a strong, yet democratic, government was possible in a country like the Congo without a democratic tradition or even a history of participation in government. Finally, after further fighting and rapine, and the seizure of the capital of Katanga by a UN force in December, Tshombe capitulated. On December 19 he signed an agreement with Premier Adoula which included a pledge to end the Katanga secession and to carry out the United Nations Resolutions.

Criticisms of the UN operation in the Congo were widespread and bitter, not only in Belgium, France, and England, but in the United States. Republicans and Democrats alike denounced our support of the action against Tshombe. To these critics, Antoine Gizenga—not Tshombe—was the real threat to the independence of the Congo. Tshombe, they argued, was strongly anti-Communist and pro-Western and thus the only Congolese leader who could prevent a Communist victory in the heart of Africa. The United States was punishing its friend and aiding its avowed enemy. There was force to this argument, and yet it ignored both the purpose of UN policy and the degree to which the UN's very existence depended on at least a qualified success of its Congo operation. UN policy was based on the correct supposition that the alternative to a strong Congolese central government was anarchy. The events of 1961 made it clear that the battle in the Congo could bring no clear victory to the UN, but it was equally obvious that defeat could make the United Nations in fact the querulously impotent thing that many of its critics would like to see it become.

Historians, looking back on 1961, may well elect to stress the significance of developments in the Common Market rather than the growing pains of the new nations.

The European Economic Community, or Common Market, is a customs union linking West Germany, France, Italy, Belgium, the Netherlands and Luxembourg. By free trade among themselves and the raising of tariff walls against outsiders, the six members have enhanced their own prosperity while making it increasingly difficult for nations like Great Britain and the United States who wish to compete in the European market. The problem was particularly serious for Great Britain who also faced the possibility of being outdistanced by the "Six" in political influence. But for Britain to seek membership in the Common Market would mean the rejection of centuries of insular aloofness and perhaps the alienation of some of her partners in the British Commonwealth. In July, as his country struggled with its sixth economic crisis since World War II, British Prime Minister Macmillan announced that he would seek membership in the Common Market. Negotiations with the other members of the Market began immediately, and although there were knotty problems to be worked out, it appeared certain that they would be resolved successfully.

Just as the emergence of the Common Market forced Britain to reconsider her position in the world, so British membership in this European Economic Community forced the United States to reappraise its foreign policy. Many Americans rejoiced in Europe's new-found strength. A few, like Mr. Walter Lippmann, came close to advocating a pooling of resources by the United States and Europe in order to raise living standards in backward areas of the world. Others endorsed a strong and united Europe because they believed it would serve as a counterweight to Russia. But a very influential segment of American opinion insisted that a mutual lowering of tariff walls between the United States and the Common Market would depress our own economy and rob Americans of jobs. President Kennedy's response to the Western Europe economic challenge was to announce his intention of asking Congress for "new and bold authority" to cut tariffs. His request undoubtedly would be the chief congressional issue of 1962.

Evaluation of Kennedy's congressional record for the year, like the assessment of his record in foreign affairs, is complicated by the wide gap between expectations and accomplishments. During the campaign and even after his election, Kennedy's emphasis on presidential leadership led his partisans to predict a second "hundred days," a repetition of the brilliant legislative record achieved by the Roosevelt administration from March-June, 1933. Such predictions and the expectations to which they led were unfortunate. The extremely narrow margin by which Kennedy won the election and the reduced majority of Democrats in the House should have been ample warning that the President's program would encounter spirited opposition. Another warning signal should have been the familiar House coalition of Conservative Republicans and Southern Democrats.

President Kennedy early realized that any immediate and ambitious reform program would be unceremoniously buried by Congress, without benefit of debate. The success of even a moderate reform program was problematical, for poised over every measure of innovation was the well-oiled guillotine wielded by the powerful House Rules Committee. It was this Committee which had defeated many of President Eisenhower's legislative proposals in 1960. More significantly, it had thwarted Senator Kennedy's attempts in August, 1960, to provide the Democratic party with a record of which he could boast during the campaign.

Kennedy's first maneuver in what was certain to be a full-fledged legislative battle was entrusted to the leader of his forces in the House, Speaker Sam Rayburn. It was a flank attack, designed to diminish the power of the six-man conservative coalition (led by Rep. Howard W. Smith of Virginia) which controlled the Rules Committee. The maneuver was simple. It was proposed to raise the Committee's membership from 12 to 15 and thus shift control from the conservative coalition to Administration forces led by Speaker Rayburn. Rep. Smith and his supporters bitterly fought the Administration's proposal, but their battle ended on January 31 when the House upheld Speaker Rayburn and President Kennedy by a margin of five votes. The narrow margin by which the deadlock was broken was an indication of the troubles the President was to have in getting his program through Congress.

On January 30, Kennedy delivered his first annual message to a joint session of Congress. The picture which he presented was a somber one; he sketched out in detail the harsh facts about the continuing struggle against the Communist powers abroad and an economic recession at home. He suggested no easy solutions to these grave perils but called on Congress and the nation to make the sacrifices necessary to meet the challenge of the crises he described. "I speak today in an hour of national peril and national opportunity," the President said. "Before my term has ended, we shall have to test anew whether a nation organized and governed such as ours can endure. The outcome is by no means certain. The answers are by no means clear. All of us together—this Administration, this Congress, this nation—must forge those answers." To deal with the recession, Kennedy promised to send Congress within two weeks a number of proposals designed to stimulate the economy. To deal with problems overseas, he proposed that the United States build more missiles and troop-carrying aircraft and thoughtfully examine and expand its foreign-aid program.

On February 2, in his annual economic message, Kennedy submitted to Congress a wide-ranging economic program. This program, many features of which had been debated in the preceding Congress, included recommendations on housing, distressed areas, Social Security benefits, a higher minimum wage, and jobless benefits.

Although many Congressmen thought that the Administration over-emphasized the seriousness of the economic recession in order to coerce Congress into granting the desired remedial measures, a majority of Congress was willing to give the President more or less what he asked. Thus an omnibus housing bill, fully meeting the President's recommendations, authorized grants for the preservation of urban open spaces, thirty five-year loan guarantees for middle-income housing, and grants and loans for development of local mass transit systems. Assistance in the redevelopment of the country's depressed areas was given by an act carrying an appropriation of $394,000,000. Social Security benefits were increased for more than 4,000,000 persons of retirement age. Although it fell short of what the President sought, a minimum-wage bill passed through both houses of Congress with surprising ease. The measure, providing for an increase in the minimum hourly rate from $1.00 to $1.25 in steps varying from two to four years, assured wage raises for millions of workers. Other emergency measures designed to give the economy a boost included payment of unemployment compensation to workers whose state benefits had run out, an increase in highway use taxes to assure completion of the 41,000-mile interstate highway system, and a public works program providing for construction of airports and water-pollution control.

Just as Congress was willing to grant first aid to a sagging economy, so it was generous in appropriating money to improve the country's military position—so generous, in fact, that it occasionally gave the President more than he requested. This generosity was the single most important factor in creating a budgetary deficit, for defense is by far the biggest item in the national budget. Thus in the $80.9 billion budget submitted by the outgoing Administration in January, Eisenhower had requested $42.8 billion for the defense establishment.

In submitting a revised budget on March 28, Kennedy requested an additional appropriation totaling $1.9 billion. Even this request, as it turned out, was not high enough, and the President was forced twice more to ask a compliant Congress for increases in the defense estimate. By the end of the session Congress had provided record peacetime outlays of $46,662,556,000 for military and civil defense and $1,671,750,000 for a space exploration program. There was money to go to the moon and money to dig shelters for protection against a possible nuclear war.

So also was there enough money for foreign aid. But in this case congressional generosity was only fiscal; it did not extend so far as acceptance of the Administration's proposals for far-reaching reforms in our foreign-aid program.

In a special message to Congress late in March, President Kennedy outlined a new philosophy and new procedures for the United States foreign-aid program. Arguing that foreign aid is essential to the security and defense of the free world against Communist encroachment and is a moral, economic and political obligation imposed on all industrially advanced free countries of the northern half of the world, he proposed that the United States enter into a partnership with other favored nations to help the peoples of underdeveloped countries break the bonds of mass misery which has blocked their advance to freedom. To this end he recommended a new unit, the Agency for International Development, and asked for authority to borrow $7.3 billion from the Treasury during the next five years to finance economic development loans. The challenge presented by the President was similar to the challenge of 1948 which had led to the Marshall Plan. The most important difference was that in 1961 the countries which had benefited from the Marshall Plan were asked to join with the United States in providing help for the non-European world. Although economy-minded Congressmen applauded the latter objective, Congress showed little evidence of the Marshall Plan spirit. The aspect of the plan to which it most strenuously objected was that which attempted to obviate an annual appeal to Congress for funds by calling for a five-year appropriation.

Although unwilling to accept *in toto* the imaginative innovations proposed by the Administration, Congress did authorize itself to appropriate $7,200,000,000 for development loans over a five-year period. The President thus acquired the authority to make long-term loan commitments in advance of appropriations, but there was no firm guarantee that the money would be appropriated. After a long and hard struggle with a spirited opposition led by Rep. Otto E. Passman of Louisiana, the customary "hatchet-man" for foreign-aid appropriations, the President also won what one spokesman termed a "satisfactory" foreign-aid appropriation of $3,914,600,000 for the fiscal year ending June 30, 1962.

The fate of the President's foreign-aid program was symptomatic of the congressional temper; it was generous yet niggardly, farsighted yet myopic. Thus Congressmen were anxious to prop up the economy, eager to provide for the country's defense, and willing to aid countries less fortunate than the United States. But they were adamantly opposed to innovation or reform, whether in foreign aid or in domestic social-welfare programs. This attitude was responsible for the defeat of health insurance for old people and government aid to education—the two domestic reform measures which headed the Administration's priority list. President Kennedy's health-insurance plan was much the same as the one which Senator Kennedy failed to get through the 86th Congress and later took to the country as candidate for the presidency. In recommending to the Congress that the program be financed by an increase in Social Security contributions, the President assured wary legislators that his plan was not the "socialized medicine" which doctors resist to the death. Nevertheless, the American Medical Association, which operates one of the strongest and toughest lobbies in Washington, resisted, and the measure was defeated by the same coalition of Republicans and Southern Conservatives who had defeated it in 1960.

Perhaps the most controversial measure proposed by the President was his plan for Federal aid to education. The 86th Congress, President Kennedy said in February, was presented an opportunity to set up a landmark in education by authorizing Federal aid to the states for their schools, something which has been talked about for forty years. He proposed that $5.6 billion be spent during the next three to five years. The largest single item in the proposal was $2.3 billion in grants to the states over the next three years for elementary and secondary school education. To these generous grants only two strings were attached. The funds were to be distributed according to the familiar formula that the states with the lowest incomes receive the most and no money was to be granted to church-supported schools. When the President presented his plan, he presumed that the chief opposition to it would come from Republicans who oppose increases in either Federal taxes or interference with the states, and from Southerners who could be counted on to oppose the bill's provision that money be withheld from tax-supported schools which maintained a color bar. The Administration miscalculated; the most effective opposition came from another quarter. The Roman Catholic hierarchy of the United States took issue with the President's plan, declaring that it would be "discriminatory" to exclude children in private schools and warning that "there would be no alternative but to oppose such discrimination." When the country's first Roman Catholic President retorted that Federal grants to church schools would violate the First Amendment to the Constitution, the battle was joined. Letters on the issue flooded congressional offices, and a heated debate—one in which religious, racial and political factors were all hopelessly mixed—raged in Congress for more than four months, not only preventing any education bill at all but holding up other parts of the President's domestic program.

Another aspect of the President's domestic program which was defeated in Congress was a new approach to the farm problem. The Administration proposed that authority be delegated to farmers and to the Secretary of Agriculture to set standards of price support and production control. Conservatives and members of the "farm bloc" retorted that the plan would usurp legislative prerogatives of Congress. Congress did make some minor changes in agricultural legislation. A bill for dealing with the 1961 crop of corn and feed grains, for example, reversed the flexible price-support policy of the Eisenhower Administration by giving the President broad authority to curtail production while maintaining high price supports. Like the unemployment compensation bill, however, these were temporary emergency measures for dealing immediately with a depressed sector of the economy. What they really meant was that the same old extravagant system of price maintenance would continue for another year.

If one were to look only at congressional emasculation of constructive measures like those for education, health, and agriculture, he well might describe the annual record of Congress with the slogan "Billions for defense but not a pittance for social reform." But such a description would leave out of account the generous and statesmanlike support which Congress gave to the President's Latin American policy, its authorization of a disarmament agency, its expansion of our cultural exchange activities and its approval of the Peace Corps which the President had set up by executive order to supply volunteer technicians and teachers to underdeveloped countries.

No policy recommended by the Kennedy Administration was more imaginative than its program for countering the deterioration of the position of the United States in Latin America. Ever since 1948 the Latin Americans had reproached the United States because they received no benefit from the Marshall Plan. In March, 1961, their reproach was heeded by the announcement of a Kennedy plan which was as broad in scope, as important, and as potentially costly as the historic Marshall Plan. Just as the latter was our answer to Stalin, so the Latin American plan was our answer to Fidel Castro. Dubbed the Alliance for Progress, it was premised on the conviction, in the President's words, that "economic progress without social progress lets the great majority of the people remain in poverty while a privileged few reap the benefits of rising abundance." Its purpose was to bring about social progress of "towering dimensions" by encouraging the Latin-American ruling classes to inaugurate land reforms and to give up some of their wealth and privileges. The President made it clear that the United States would be prepared to lend or give money only to those countries whose ruling classes had shown themselves ready to cooperate in this effort of self-sacrifice. More specifically, the plan called for a ten-year multi-billion dollar plan to raise the living standards of all Latin Americans, provide basic education, end hunger, and place each nation on a basis of self-sustaining growth. The President proposed as "a first step" that Congress appropriate $500,000,000 which the United States had promised Latin Americans at the Bogotá Conference in 1960.

Congress quickly granted the President what he asked. Because of the possibilities it offered for Latin-American growth and prosperity, the plan was obviously of major historic importance. It was important, too, in demonstrating the nimbleness with which the President and his advisers adapted their policies to Latin America's needs. On August 17, the Alliance for Progress became a reality. At Punta del Este, Uruguay, delegates from all the Latin-American nations except Cuba ratified the basic charter of the Alliance. The United States delegation—led by Treasury Secretary Douglas Dillon—presented a program which offered direct United States aid of at least $1.1 billion a year and $900 million from other sources. This figure should be contrasted with the total of $3.5 billion granted to Latin American countries from 1945 to 1960.

At dawn of September 27, the House of Representatives forced adjournment over the protests of a frustrated Senate. Despite reports that President Kennedy was thoroughly satisfied with the session's achievements, it was clear that Congress had balked at the very outset of the trip to the New Frontier.

If Kennedy failed to fulfill the great expectations which had been held for his Administration in political and international affairs, he more than fulfilled them in economic affairs. The recession which was becoming increasingly serious as he took office and about which he devoted so many messages to Congress ended by midyear. The reversal, indeed, was so swift that by December the spectre of runaway inflation again was dominating the thought of most economists.

In the last weeks of 1960 the professional collectors of dark economic omens had no shortage of material. Steel production was at a very low level; automobile inventories were high; the drain on U. S. gold stocks was continuing; government officials were freely predicting that unemployment would shortly reach the five or six million mark. But economic optimists could point to other economic facts which suggested that the slump was a mild one. Employment was high, and the gross national product had just crossed $500 billion a year for the first time. The national economy, in brief, was full of paradoxes.

As Kennedy took office three basic economic problems confronted him. The first was the recession. The second, and more serious one, was an apparent slowdown in the country's rate of economic growth which was marked by a persistently high unemployment rate. Unemployment in January, for example, was 5,400,000, the highest of any January since World War II. Allied to this problem was the rapid deterioration of conditions in chronically depressed communities where the plight of many thousands was as severe as it had been during the Great Depression. The third basic problem was a balance of payments crisis, arising from the fact that the United States' spending abroad recently had exceeded United States' earnings by about $4 billion a year. This situation had created a drain of the nation's gold reserve and raised questions about the continued stability of the dollar.

In dealing with the third problem, the Kennedy Administration made few shifts in either tactics or strategy from the program of the previous Administration. The plan which the President announced to Congress early in February was essentially Mr. Eisenhower's blueprint. Nevertheless (and for a variety of reasons too complex to discuss here), the battle to defend the dollar was moderately successful, for the total loss of gold in 1961 was about one-half of the annual average loss for the last three years. On the second problem, all the ingenuity of the President's economic advisers and all the efforts of Congress could not put together again the Humpty Dumpty of unemployment. The first problem, whether because of Administration measures or not, was a true Cinderella story. By December, a drab and sluggish economy had turned into a spectacular boom.

From the low point of the recession which was reached in the first two months of the year, the economy quickly rebounded. By April the signs of an upturn were evident; by May they were unmistakable. Thus the Federal Reserve Board's index of industrial production (the most important of some thirty government indicators which together give a picture of the national economy) rose from a low point of 102 in January and February to an impressive 105 in April (the index, which uses 1957 as the base year, had reached 110 in May, 1960, the recognized point at which the recession began). In May it moved up to 108, and in July set a new record of 112. Economic activity was expanding on practically every front. The stock market reflected the economy's resurgence by reaching a new high; personal income reached a record; construction was climbing at a rapid pace; the gross national product rose in the second quarter (April-June) by $15.3 billion to an annual rate of $516.1 billion, also a record. All these statistics indicated that the recession of 1960-61 was the mildest of the four postwar recessions.

Unquestionably, some of the credit for the rapid recovery was due to the Administration. It gained the cooperation of the Federal Reserve authorities whose easy money policy provided the funds for expansion. And it took a number of steps, as we have seen, which helped to promote the recovery. Government spending, for example, was pushed up substantially, with the result that the budget, which was showing a surplus in mid-1960, was showing a deficit by mid-1961. At the same time, spending by state and local authorities increased, partly as a result of Federal measures.

Throughout the remaining months of 1961 the economy gained momentum. Although the spectacular advances of the second quarter of the year were not matched in the third, the pace of recovery accelerated in the final months of the year. By November, the *New York Times'* combined average of fifty representative stocks reached 411.17, coming within striking distance of the 1959 record high; automobile production increased; there were gains in business investment; the index of industrial production reached a new high; and corporate profits and personal income were rising.

In the midst of this boom, however, the nettlesome problem of unemployment persisted. In July, as so many indices of prosperity soared zestfully upward, the percentage of the labor force without jobs remained 6.9, unchanged from its recession high. In October the Labor Department announced that unemployment fell, in absolute numbers, below four million for the first time in a year. But the same report included the somber information that unemployment continued at 6.8 percent, making October the eleventh consecutive month in which the rate had hovered around 7 percent.

In the opinion of Administration economists, full employment, which would mean an unemployment rate of no more than 4 percent, could be achieved only through expansion of the economy. But such expansion would raise anew the problem of inflation, that persistent problem which, like unemployment itself, has threatened the American economy for many years.

In the field of Negro rights the year 1961 saw a continuation of the snail-like advances which have been made over the last decade and a half. Depending on one's viewpoint, these advances either represent the triumph of gradualism—the slow and steady progress which in the long run accomplishes major changes without the dangers and dislocations often brought by swift change—or they indicate the almost ineluctable barrier to urgently needed reform which can be created by a determined minority which wraps itself in the banner of states' rights.

In the eight years which have passed since the Supreme Court ruled that the country's public schools must proceed to integrate white and Negro children "with all deliberate speed," at least token integration has taken place in all states which formerly practiced segregation except Alabama, Mississippi, and South Carolina. The familiar pattern has been token integration accompanied by sporadic violence; thus states like Maryland and North Carolina have admitted the minimum number of Negro children necessary to ward off further decrees by the Federal courts, while in other states even this limited desegregation has precipitated violence, as in Clinton, Tenn., in 1956, Little Rock, Ark., in 1957, and New Orleans, La., in 1960. In the year 1961 the pattern slightly shifted, for there was token and peaceful integration in several Southern areas. Dallas became the last large city in Texas to integrate; Florida, Louisiana, and Virginia opened additional schools to Negroes; in New Orleans integration showed slow but orderly gains. In all, a total of eighteen Southern school districts moved toward integration for the first time, although only an estimated 500 Negro pupils were involved. By September, 801 out of the 2,813 biracial school districts in seventeen Southern and border states and the District of Columbia had achieved some degree of integration.

Emphasis on integration of the public schools has tended to obscure the history of integration in the nation's colleges and universities. Since the University of Maryland first broke through the barrier of racial segregation by admitting a Negro student to its law school in 1936, the number of Negroes in Southern institutions of higher learning steadily has increased. Thus by 1961, 118 of the 211 formerly all-white institutions were technically integrated. This progress, however, has not been so spectacular as a cursory glance at these statistics would suggest. In the seventeen Southern and border states there are more than 500,000 white students in tax-supported universities and only about 5,000 Negroes in classes with them. In some of the desegregated universities, furthermore, Negroes are admitted only to graduate or professional schools. The result is that most Negroes who wish to go to college in the South must continue to attend all-Negro colleges, institutions at which educational opportunity is inferior in almost all respects.

This situation was forcefully brought to public attention in January, 1961, by the admission, under a court order, of two Negro students to the University of

Georgia—the first crack in that state's pattern of total racial segregation in education. State officials were relatively restrained in speech and action, and the two Negro students seemed to have won the quiet acceptance of their classmates. Then, suddenly, and evidently with outside instigation, rioting flared and the two Negroes were "temporarily" suspended by the University "for their own safety." The Negroes were soon readmitted, owing to the order of a Federal judge and the conclusion of Georgia officials that they would rather have a little integration than a closed university.

The most important advance in integration during the year, however, was not in education; nor was it due to the orders of Federal courts. The successful attack on segregation in public transportation and in public terminals, like the success of the lunch-counter demonstrations in 1960, was carried out by individuals (Negro and white) to whom the long and lumbering process of change through litigation is intolerable.

Early in May a group of biracial "Freedom Riders," sponsored by the Congress on Racial Equality, a militant civil rights group, boarded regularly scheduled interstate buses to test racial practices at stations in the Deep South. On May 20, serious violence erupted when they arrived in Birmingham, the capital of Alabama. More than two dozen of them were beaten by mobs at the bus station, a flagrant example of lawlessness during which the Birmingham police force found it convenient to be elsewhere. When Gov. John Patterson proved uncooperative, Atty. Gen. Robert Kennedy dispatched more than 400 armed U. S. marshals and deputies to the scene, the first use of Federal forces to curb segregationist violence since President Eisenhower ordered troops to Little Rock, Ark., in 1957. Confronted by Federal troops and martial law, state and local officials soon decided to make an all-out effort to preserve order.

Undeterred by the violence in Birmingham, another group of Freedom Riders, traveling in heavily guarded buses, carried the antisegregationists' fight into Jackson, the capital of Mississippi, and a center of militant segregationists. In sharp contrast to their reception in Birmingham, the Freedom Riders were protected at the Jackson terminal by 300 soldiers and police. But when they sought service at the "white" cafeteria or entered "white" rest rooms, they were arrested and at subsequent hearings were fined and given suspended jail sentences. That the Freedom Riders could enter Jackson without encountering violence would not have been predicted a month earlier by the most serene of optimists. Atty. Gen. Kennedy's resoluteness in sending Federal marshals to restore law and order in Birmingham presumably forced the State of Mississippi, however sullenly, to take precautions for the safety of the riders. Kennedy then counseled moderation, urging travelers to stay out of Alabama and Mississippi until "reason and normalcy have been restored." At the same time, however, he asked the Interstate Commerce Commission to put teeth into its antisegregation statutes and, as result, the ICC handed down on September 22 a new ruling, prohibiting interstate bus and railroad companies from using segregated terminals. When the new ruling went into effect, there were incidents of violence in several places in the South.

The Freedom Riders demonstrated anew how difficult it is for even the best-organized and most courageous crusaders to make a dent in the solid wall of Southern resistance to racial integration. But they also demonstrated that it is possible to carve steps in that wall which later reformers may use to scale it. The riders made it clear that the Southern states are not always prepared to challenge Federal authority; it was apparent even to Mississippians that local feeling, however strong, cannot prevail in a test of physical strength with the Federal government. This also had been the lesson of Little Rock. The invasion of Mississippi may not have been quite the historic step that some liberals acclaimed it to be, but it was clearly a significant one in the unfolding of Negro protest.

The Supreme Court settled in 1961 the question of the constitutionality of two pieces of legislation dealing with communism with which it had struggled for many years. One was the membership clause of the Smith Act of 1940 which makes it a crime to be a member of a group advocating the overthrow of the government. The other legislation was the Internal Security Act of 1950 which required Communist "action" and "front" groups to register and list their officers and members. Once it registered, an organization was subject to severe sanctions; its members could not use or even apply for a passport; it would lose tax exemptions; it would be required to stamp its mail "Disseminated by ————, a Communist organization"; and its members were barred from government employment.

The most important of the Smith Act cases involved Junius I. Scales, a former Communist leader in North Carolina who was first sentenced in 1955. Scales' counsel argued that the membership clause of the Smith Act limited freedom of speech and association in violation of the First Amendment. This statute, the argument ran, covered not actual attempts at the overthrow of the government but membership in a group that merely advocated overthrow, however unlikely success seemed to be. Speaking for a five-man majority, Justice John Marshall Harlan rejected this argument on the grounds that it already had been disposed of by the Court in the Dennis case of 1951—a case in which the Supreme Court upheld the conviction of party leaders under the Smith Act for conspiring to advocate the overthrow of the government. The extent of division on the Court in this case was reflected in a dissent by Justice William O. Douglas. "Nothing but beliefs are on trial in this case," he said. "They are unpopular and to most of us revolting. But they are nonetheless ideas or dogmas of faith within the broad framework of the First Amendment. What we lose by majority vote today may be reclaimed at a future time when the fear of advocacy, dissent and non-con-formity no longer cast a shadow over us."

In the case involving the Internal Security Act of 1950, the Supreme Court sustained a finding of the Subversive Activities Control Board that the Communist party is an "action" organization under the Act and that it is required to register and to list the names of all its officers and members. The Court refused, however, to pass on the constitutionality of the penalties, saying such questions were premature. Justice Frankfurter, speaking for himself and Justices Clark, Harlan, Whittaker and Stewart, found no violation of the First Amendment's guarantees of free speech and association in the requirement to register and list members. He also cited findings by Congress that the Communist party is controlled from abroad and uses "methods of infiltration and secretive and coercive tactics," that "a Communist network exists in the United States," and that Communist agents practice sabotage and espionage. Justice Frankfurter concluded that "it is not for the courts to re-examine the validity of these legislative findings and reject them." Only Justice Black dissented from this opinion on First Amendment grounds.

Just as the Court restricted the meaning of the First Amendment in cases involving Communists, so also it refused to see in that Amendment any bar to movie censorship. The case involved Chicago's film censorship system in which all movies have to be brought to the Police Department for inspection before the necessary permit is issued. A five-man majority held that guarantees of free speech do not mean the right to show any and every film, no matter how objectionable, at least once. The Court's division on this case was the same as on the Communist cases: The majority consisted of Justices Clark, Frankfurter, Harlan, Whittaker and Stewart; in the minority were Chief Justice Warren, Justices Black, Douglas, and Brennan. The dissenters denounced the decision in strong language as a "retreat" from free speech, warning that it might lead to licensing and censorship of not only films, but also newspapers and books. This same minority spoke even more vigorously in protest against a number of decisions which upheld in broad terms the investigating powers of the House Committee on Un-American Activities. The dissenting justices charged that in confirming the contempt convictions of two critics of the House group (Frank Wilkinson and Carl Broden) who refused to testify about possible Communist affiliations, the Court had opened the way for the House committee to intimidate its critics by investigating them.

If the Justices were divided on many issues of freedom of speech, belief and association, they were unanimous, or nearly so, in demanding fair play for American Negroes. The Supreme Court unanimously struck down a Louisiana law which required the National Association for the Advancement of Colored People to list all local members and swear that no national officers were members of "subversive" groups. It held that a privately operated restaurant situated in a publicly owned parking garage in Wilmington, Del., could not refuse to serve Negroes. In another decision, the Court said that bus terminal restaurants operated as "an integral part" of interstate bus service and might not segregate passengers. Finally, the Court unanimously affirmed lower court decisions, which had held that Louisiana's various efforts to block the desegregation of schools in New Orleans were unconstitutional.

The record-breaking number of decisions handed down by the Supreme Court in 1961 included not only civil rights cases but cases on a wide diversity of subjects. Its rulings ranged from one upholding state "blue laws" to one which sanctioned a Florida law making jury duty voluntary for women while it was compulsory for men. Among its many decisions the following were of particular interest or importance: In an Ohio case involving one Dollree Mapp, the Court forbade state courts to admit evidence in criminal cases which had been secured illegally. Such evidence had been barred from Federal courts since 1914, but to extend the prohibition to state judicial procedure meant overturning a decision handed down by the Supreme Court itself in 1949 (Wolf v. Colorado). Some students of the Court described this ruling as the most significant limitation ever imposed on state criminal procedure in a single decision by the Supreme Court. It was certain to have sweeping effects on local law enforcement. Indicating the unpredictability of Court decisions, seven of the Justices upheld the right of the states to use wire tap evidence, even though it is obtained in a manner contrary to Federal law. In this case, the Court refused to alter a 1928 ruling which held that wire tapping is not a "search" and hence is not subject to constitutional restrictions. In another decision the Justices ruled that the Railway Labor Act which requires railway workers to join trade unions in order to hold their jobs was not to be interpreted as authorizing the use of their dues for political purposes of which they disapproved. In one of the greatest antitrust cases in its history, the Court ruled that E. I. du Pont de Nemours & Co. had to dispose of its 63,000,000 shares in the General Motors Corp. The Court directed that divestiture of the shares (amounting to almost $3,000,000,000) begin immediately and be completed within ten years. In still another antitrust action, the Court unanimously rejected the suit brought by truckers against the railroads for conspiring to prejudice the Pennsylvania legislature against trucks. Lobbying, the Court said, might be a great evil but it was not an antitrust violation.

It may well be that historians a century from now will pay only perfunctory attention to the subjects which have dominated this annual survey of events. "The Kennedy Era," the "Cold War," the "Age of Anxiety," all these terms which are frequently used to describe the contemporary scene may give way in their books to the term "The Space Age." Only four years after the first man-made satellite went into orbit, James E. Webb, administrator of the National Aeronautics and Space Administration could write: "Space is becoming the focal area for the major scientific and technological disciplines. At the same time, highly important lines of development in economics, education, and international affairs are converging on space exploration and its supporting activities." These significant developments were dramatized in 1961 by man's first flights into space.

On April 12, Moscow radio announced that: "The world's first space ship Vostok, with a man on board, was placed in an around-the-earth orbit in the Soviet Union. The pilot space navigator . . . is a citizen of the USSR, Flight Maj. Yuri Alekseyevich Gagarin." According to Moscow, Maj. Gagarin was within minutes in an orbit ranging from 109 to 188 miles above the earth and traveling at a speed above 17,000 miles an hour —far higher and faster than any human had ever traveled. Whatever its implications for the US-USSR military and political rivalry, the Soviet triumph represented a spectacular achievement in the exploration of space and an exciting milestone on the way to interplanetary travel.

The astronautical feats of Maj. Gagarin inaugurated a lively space race between the United States and Russia. He was followed in the stratosphere by three other explorers, two Americans and one Russian. On May 5, an American astronaut hurtled into space and came down to a safe landing. Comdr. Alan B. Shepard's flight did not equal the Russian achievement, but it gave the nation a psychological lift as was evident from the tremendous reception he got from the President, Congress, the press, and the public.

On July 21, the third chapter of the man-in-space drama was enacted when Capt. Virgil I. Grissom, another American, soared 100 miles high above the earth in a flight that was almost an exact duplicate of the one made by Comdr. Shepard. The year's fourth astronaut performed the most spectacular feat of all. At Moscow's Vnukovo Airport on August 9, Maj. Gherman Stepanovitch Titov strode to a platform full of Soviet notables, saluted Premier Khrushchev and declared: "Comrade First Secretary of the Central Committee . . . the assignment has been completed. On the sixth and seventh of August, 1961, I carried out a twenty-five-hour space flight in the spaceship Vostok II. I orbited the earth seventeen times and landed safely in the pre-determined area. . . ." Maj. Titov's multiple-orbit flight was the longest journey yet taken by man; 437,500 miles, or nearly the distance to the moon and back.

While these feats of man in space teased the public imagination with hints of even more exciting solar expeditions yet to come, one other possibility of the uses of space created widespread public alarm. Whether to build or not to build fall-out shelters for protection against atomic warfare agitated the American public in 1961. The problem was one of protection against the deadly radioactive dust which descends like rain after a nuclear attack, for it is agreed that no one within several

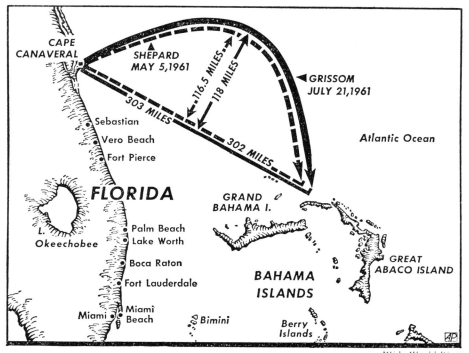

CAPE
CANAVERAL

SHEPARD
MAY 5,1961

116.5 MILES

118 MILES

303 MILES

302 MILES

GRISSOM
JULY 21,1961

Atlantic Ocean

Sebastian

Vero Beach

Fort Pierce

FLORIDA

GRAND
BAHAMA I.

L.
Okeechobee

Palm Beach
Lake Worth

Boca Raton

Fort Lauderdale

Miami
Beach

Miami

Bimini

**BAHAMA
ISLANDS**

GREAT
ABACO ISLAND

Berry
Islands

Wide World Photo

Diagram showing comparative distances and altitudes of sub-orbital flights of Captain
Grissom and Commander Shepard

miles of the immediate blast of a bomb can survive. Fall-
out shelters made daily appearances on the front page of
newspapers as well as in advertisements and public displays of the food and other equipment which should go
in them promoted items like portable, pocket-size kits
to measure radiation. The government's booklet on how
to build your own shelters was being distributed by mid-
October at a rate of 500,000 copies a week, and *Life*
magazine sold out an issue which featured the same information. Public controversy centered on the question

of the extent to which shelters would afford protection and on the problem of whether they should be built at the expense of individuals or of the Federal government.

To future historians of the American social scene the dispute during the year over fall-out shelters may appear to have been a new manifestation of popular anxieties created by the Space Age. Other aspects of the social scene in 1961 doubtless will not be considered unique but will be treated as but a part of the changing nature of American society in the decades after World War II. Thus it perhaps will be recorded that the percentage of women in the working population continued to increase as it had done since 1940. In July, 1961, a third of American workers were women; this represented a rise of almost a million over July of the previous year. It may also be recorded that the number of "white-collar workers" continued to increase. A study published in 1961 by the Department of Labor pointed out that about half the working Americans not employed on farms are now members of the white-collar force and predicted that by 1970 the group will increase by about nine million.

Future historians may also stress the extent to which an abundant economy was altering the recreational habits of the American people: For example, it may be reported that week-end boating (a sport which requires money to spend and leisure time to spend it in) was the largest and the fastest growing outdoor sport in the

United States in 1961 as in the years immediately before. Again, it may be reported that television continued to be the favorite indoor recreation of Americans. In 1961, there were approximately 55,500,000 television sets in the country. For future readers who might deplore this trend, the historian could balance his account by relating that the enormous increase in the production and sale of paperback books meant that more Americans were buying books than ever before. In 1961, his account might state, well over 1,000,000 paperbacks a day were bought. The type of paperbacks which were bought, moreover, were not only those dealing with "sex, sadism and the smoking gun" but works on religions, philosophy, science, history and literature.

In general, American publishers of books were inclined to look forward to a more or less golden future, a state of mind which may or may not be justified when our future historians study the record. The rapidly increasing population of the nation's schools and colleges encouraged textbook publishers in particular to optimism, and to a vast proliferation of product. In the field of pure literature and scholarship, among events worthy of notice were the death of Ernest Hemingway on July 2, which appeared to many the end of an era in American writing, and the publication of the earliest volumes of the collected papers of John Adams and Alexander Hamilton, two long-range ventures which had been many years in preparation. Civil War enthusiasts continued to be offered a variety of books which ranged from serious and well-documented university studies to shameless catering to a vogue and several excellent works examined the mounting problems of the American city considered as a social and economic entity.

THE RECORD OF 1962

T HE major emphasis of the Kennedy Administration in the year 1962 was on domestic rather than on foreign affairs. This was not because the cold war abated or because our major foreign problems were settled. It was rather owing to a stalemate in our relations with Russia. Except for the bold and successful effort of the United States to thwart Soviet imperialism in the Caribbean, the two countries shied away from the brink of global war. They were thus freer than in the past to deal with urgent national problems (Khrushchev with sagging agricultural production, Kennedy with a sluggish economy) and to try to mend deteriorating relations with allies (Khrushchev with Communist China, Kennedy with France and West Germany).

This emphasis on domestic affairs was reflected in the President's annual message to Congress. Kennedy did not minimize our overseas problems, but he did emphasize constructive solutions to our problems at home. That he could do so suggests that a balance of power, however shaky, has been established between East and West, leaving the United States free to concentrate its attention on improving the nation's health and its educational system, on eradicating its glaring social inequalities, on strengthening its economy, and on cementing its partnership with the rapidly developing nations of the free world.

The recurrent theme of the President's message was that domestic and foreign issues are intertwined. We must "fulfill the world's hope by fulfilling our own faith," he said, and went on to recommend job training and tax incentives, rehabilitation rather than relief, medical insurance and improved schools. The specific proposals which he made, however, were neither novel nor new; they were substantially the same as those which he had recommended in 1961. Even so, most Congressmen viewed much of his legislative program as a glittering prospectus of goals unlikely to be achieved in 1962, if ever.

On foreign relations the President reviewed our international problems, emphasizing our difficulties in Berlin, in the Congo, in the United Nations, in Southeast Asia, and in Latin America. The aspect of foreign affairs which he highlighted, however, was the relationship of the United States to the European Common Market. To meet the challenge of an economically rejuvenated Europe, he called for a new and bold American trade policy.

In his annual budget message the President converted the ideas expressed in his annual message into dollars and cents. For fiscal 1963—the year beginning July 1, 1962, and ending June 30, 1963—he proposed outlays of $92.5 billion, the highest budget since fiscal 1945 (when spending reached $98.7 billion). A gauge of the importance of the defense effort to the American economy was the

58

amount requested for national defense. This sum (including appropriations requested for international and space programs) accounted for more than three-fifths of the total and for more than three-fourths of the increase over 1962. Kennedy defended this increase on the grounds that the United States must not only maintain its nuclear arsenal but must also build up its conventional forces.

The requested appropriations for domestic affairs were a clear expression of the Administration's social and economic philosophy. Although the total requested was substantially unchanged from the previous year, the President pointed out that there were "important shifts in direction and emphasis." One such shift was a reduction of about $500 million in the projected spending for farm programs; another was an increase of $800 million for education, health, and welfare.

Kennedy could not have been unaware of the difficulties which his program would encounter in the second session of the 87th Congress. The Democratic majorities were impressive on paper, but they could not be relied on to push through the President's program. Under Kennedy as under Eisenhower, the Congress was in fact controlled by a coalition of Southern Democrats and conservative Republicans. The business of the 87th Congress, as of every Congress for a generation or more, was conducted through a maze of some 250 committees and subcommittees, which created confusion and made it difficult to pinpoint responsibility.

Underlying the contest between Kennedy and Congress was a basic disagreement on what American problems are and what the American future should be. Congress represents to a large extent the presuppositions and ideals of rural and small-town America, while President Kennedy represents the needs of urban America. The disagreement between them is, in one sense, a contest between the past and the present, for congressional action is often geared to an America which disappeared in the dust raised up by the half-century long trek from country to city. At the beginning of the century, about 40% of Americans lived in cities; today 75% of all Americans live in the vast conglomerations of metropolis and suburbia. This urbanization is but one of the changes that has transformed the United States in the past few decades. Scientific, political, economic and social "revolutions" also have created problems that do not yield to the formulas of yesterday. The results of these problems are obvious enough—they are revealed in population figures, unemployment figures, school statistics, and in countless other ways. Their solution just as obviously depends on imaginative new programs, not on repeating the stereotypes of the past.

How did President Kennedy deal with these problems? The predominant trait of his Administration was to seek out problems and propose solutions (even where no problems existed, or no solutions were possible, his detractors said). Messages, letters, and proposed bills flowed from the White House in an endless stream. Presidential news conferences were filled with phrases like "we hope," "move ahead," "take action," and "new opportunities." Congress was consistently prodded by the recommendation of measures which would aid large numbers of Americans and which had wide popular support—increased compensation for the unemployed, mass inoculation for children, college scholarships and job training, consumer aids, better housing, and medical care.

But the Administration's attempt to sweeten the congressional reform pill with a generous coating of popular appeal was not notably successful. The President's requests for a department of urban affairs, and for the modernization of the nation's deteriorating transportation system, his recommendations for medical care for the aged, for aid to education, and for reform of the government's farm policy, his plea for an overhaul of unemployment insurance and for action to ward off future recessions through tax cuts and large-scale public works—all were denied. But the Congress, while denying the President all that he wanted, did accept a part of his domestic program. And in legislation relating to foreign affairs and appropriations for national defense, it was willing to grant whatever he asked.

One of the most needed reforms urged on the Congress was the creation of a cabinet post for urban affairs. As the President reminded Congress, the country's urban areas contain three-quarters of the country's population and (although the President did not say so) it was obvious that to deny them the representation enjoyed by the farmers, the laborers and the businessmen at the cabinet table was as unfair as it was undemocratic. But to ask the Congress to admit such a principle was to ask it to denounce the very basis of its selection, for the rural areas of the country are grossly overrepresented in Congress. The President's program was defeated by a heavy one-sided vote scarcely a month after it was introduced in Congress. Kennedy was doubtless correct in insisting that the creation of such a department was inevitable and that congressional opposition to it was largely sectional. The accuracy of his prediction was rendered more likely only a month after the bill's defeat when the Supreme Court handed down a decision which may, in years to come, drastically curtail the influence of rural constituencies in the councils of state and nation.

The term "historic decision" has become the common currency of American journalists and newscasters in describing the work of the Supreme Court. However abused the term, it is applicable to Baker v. Carr, a decision handed down by the Court on March 26. The lawsuit involved was brought by a group of Tennessee city dwellers who, like many other urbanites, believed that their interests had been frustrated by rural control of the state legislature. The Tennessee legislature had not been reapportioned since 1901, despite provisions in the state constitution requiring reapportionment every ten years. After an unsuccessful suit in the state courts, the urban forces took their case to a three-judge Federal District Court. That Court agreed that the plaintiff's rights had been violated, but it said "the remedy does not lie with the courts." The lower court based its refusal to act on a succession of Supreme Court decisions beginning with the landmark case of Colegrave v. Green in 1946.

Speaking for a majority of six justices, Justice William J. Brennan, Jr., in effect overruled the doctrine of the Colegrave case. He held that the Federal courts had the power, and the duty, to consider the constitutionality of state legislative apportionments. Apportionments could be so unfair, the Court said, as to violate the clause of the Fourteenth Amendment providing that no state shall "deny to any person . . . the equal protection of the laws." The Court sent the case back to the three-judge Federal bench in Tennessee for a decision on the constitutionality of the present Tennessee legislative districts. The prevailing view in Washington was that the decision would not produce immediate political changes of significance.

That appraisal could not have been more mistaken. In the months after the Tennessee decision nothing less than a political revolution was begun. Lower Federal courts plunged in where the Supreme Court feared to tread, informing state legislatures that they must redistrict at once. State courts began to follow the Federal lead. Maryland's highest court, for example, all but invited the Governor to call a special session of the legislature; Kentucky's Governor filed his own lawsuit asking the courts to tell him what he ought to do. Other Governors called special sessions and urged the legislators to redistrict before the courts did it for them. Within six weeks after the Supreme Court's decision, legal or political action looking towards redistricting had begun in twenty-six states.

The zeal with which judges and politicians acted on the Supreme Court's somewhat restricted decision was astonishing. But to predict a political millennium surely would be premature. For one thing, it should be remembered that rural politicians are powerful, shrewd, and tenacious. It is questionable, moreover, how much equality in legislative districts the Supreme Court will hold the Constitution to require. But if problems remained, at least it was clear that the process of reform had at last begun.

As rural legislators closed ranks to defend their political existence, the congressional representatives of rural constituencies marshaled votes to thwart the President's program. By early April, Congress, in session for three months, had passed only one major bill dealing with domestic affairs—a multi-million dollar job-retraining program. Of the many bills still before the Congress, the most important were those dealing with six important subjects: food and drug control, taxes, farms, aid to education, medical care for the aged, and trade.

The Drug Industry Act of 1962 was more in response to popular pressure than to presidential persuasion. In mid-March Kennedy sent the Congress a message on protection of consumers who, he said, "are the only important group in the country who are not effectively organized." The President called for a tightening of food and drug controls and other regulatory practices, more information for consumers from federal sources, and a new Consumer Advisory Council. Despite the energetic efforts of Sen. Estes Kefauver to promote the bill, it languished in committee.

"There Ought to Be a Law"

Hungerford
in *The Pittsburgh Post-Gazette*

There it might have remained had not the urgent need for reform been dramatically demonstrated by the pernicious effects of a new drug, thalidomide. It was demonstrated that if taken during pregnancy thalidomide might cause deformities in unborn infants. Although the courageous obstinacy of Dr. Frances Kelsey of the Federal Food and Drug Administration kept the new sedative off the American market, it had been given to several hundred people experimentally before being withdrawn in March, 1962, and other Americans had purchased the drug abroad.

The bitter lesson of thalidomide strengthened the hands of Sen. Kefauver and the result was the Drug Industry Act of 1962, a measure which strengthened the Food and Drug Administration's power to prevent the commercial marketing of a new product until it has been approved, and which increased its power to inspect and regulate the production, labeling, and advertising of drugs and the information about them which is given to doctors.

Unfortunately for President Kennedy, his economic reform program received no such popular boost as that which put over the drug bill. The Administration's economic proposals were based on the President's diagnosis of the country's economy and his prescription for its continued health. Although the performance of the economy was diagnosed as reasonably good, he was disturbed by the country's slow rate of economic growth over the past decade and by the resulting high rate of unemployment and numerous areas of chronic depression. The President was also concerned about ways of coping with future recessions. As he pointed out, recovery from each of the four recessions in the United States since World War II (recessions beginning in November, 1948, July, 1953, July, 1957, and May, 1960) has been successively slower. For example, by January, 1962, the latest recovery had been in process twenty months and signs indicated continued sluggishness. To obviate another protracted recession, Kennedy asked Congress to provide him with a number of palliatives and reforms, among them standby tax-cutting authority, authorization to inaugurate public-works projects, and improvement of the unemployment compensation system. He also requested a tax revision designed to spur business investment in equipment, approval of a plan for a withholding system for income from interest and dividends, and curbs on expense-account deductions.

Congress was finally to give the President a small part of what he asked for—it would endorse his request for a 7% tax credit to business firms for investment in new equipment, and go part way in granting his request for restrictions on expense-account deductions. But both the Administration's economic program and the congressional debate on it were overshadowed from April on by two important economic events. The first was a battle between the President and the steel industry over increased steel prices which intensified business distrust of the Administration; the second was a sharp decline in stock prices which left many stockholders wondering whether they would have any dividends to declare under the President's proposed withholding system.

The dispute between the United States government and the steel industry was the unfortunate climax to what had been heralded as the economic success story of the year 1962. The contract between the eleven major steel companies and the 430,000 employees represented by the United Steelworkers would expire on June 30. On February 15, thanks to pressure from President Kennedy, negotiations got off to an early start in Pittsburgh, the steel capital. To the President it was important to avoid a strike which would check economic recovery in 1962 as the long steel strike in 1959 had checked the recovery in that year. He also considered it important to ensure that the settlement in steel (which was sure to set a precedent for other labor negotiations during the year) would not be inflationary, and that it would not slow down economic growth by making substantial cuts in hours of labor.

Late in March it appeared that the Administration had won a notable victory. The negotiators in Pittsburgh reached an agreement which provided that there should be no increase in wages during the first year of a two-year contract. In return for this concession, labor secured higher unemployment benefits, pensions, and more paid holidays for long-service workers. It was estimated that the costs of these concessions would be 10 cents an hour for each worker. The President hailed this noninflationary wage settlement as "industrial statesmanship of the highest order," and assumed that there would be no increase in the price of steel.

But on April 9, Roger M. Blough, head of the United States Steel Corporation, informed President Kennedy that the company was raising its price immediately by $6 per ton and that an announcement to that effect had already been sent to the press. Within hours after the announcement by U. S. Steel, five other steel companies increased their prices $6 a ton. How would the Administration react to the industry's violation of what the Administration assumed had been an agreement between the workers and the companies to promote the national interest by a noninflationary settlement? The United States economy in April, 1962, was in a mixed phase; profits were believed to be higher than at any time since the Korean War, and it was predicted that the year 1962 would compare with the fabulous boom year of 1955. But at the same time the rate of unemployment was hovering around 5½%. The Administration, aware that the steel strike in 1959 had reversed an economic upswing, had hoped that the steel settlement would pave the way in 1962 for a continued, if modest, upturn.

His hopes thus rudely disappointed, President Kennedy was bitter and infuriated at what he called the steel producers' "utter contempt" for all Americans (and himself) in their pursuit of "private power and profit." To forestall the increase, the President brought out all the big guns from the Executive arsenal—public denunciation, pressure to split industry ranks, the threat of loss of government contracts, and moves toward criminal prosecution under the antitrust laws. The possibility of forcing the steel companies to rescind the price increase centered on the success of the Administration's efforts to persuade those companies (controlling about 30% of the country's steel capacity) which had not gone along with U. S. Steel to hold the price line. Mr. Blough had admitted that there would be difficulties if these companies held out. They did, and on April 13, with the Administration's pressure against the increase gathering force, Bethlehem Steel, the country's second largest producer, agreed to price stability. U. S. Steel capitulated on the same day, only 72 hours after it had precipitated the price-increase parade, and the other steel companies quickly fell into line.

The outcome was scarcely surprising, for it was obvious (to everyone except perhaps Mr. Blough) that the United States government is bigger than U. S. Steel. The timing of the price increase, the manner in which it was announced to the President, the obvious collusion between U. S. Steel and other steel companies, the popular belief (whether true or not) that the steel executives had gone back on their word—all these things seriously damaged the public image of Big Steel. This is not to say that the argument of the steel industry should have been lightly dismissed. The steel plants of the country were in urgent need of modernization, a need reflected in the comparative figures on United States and European steel production. From 1954-60 steel production in the United States rose by 10%; in the same period the six nations of the European Common Market increased their steel production 66%. To put the problem another way, the United States' share of world steel trade had dropped from 17% to about 7% in ten years. But if the steel companies' argument for a price increase was persuasive, the government's argument for price stability was even more forceful. An increase in steel prices would obviously affect the price of most other goods, and any nudge toward inflation would make United States exports harder to sell at a time of sharply increasing competition from West Europe and Japan and in the face of a persistent deficit in the balance of United States payments.

The business community scarcely had time to recover from what many of its members regarded as a shocking demonstration of the government's willingness to dominate the economy, private as well as public, when it was faced with a sharp and sudden drop in security prices. On May 28 prices on Wall Street fell more sharply than at any time since October, 1929. Previous declines in the long postwar bull market had been infrequent and limited to less than 10%. But the 1962 dive in share prices, which brought a reduction of over 25% in the Dow-Jones industrial index, was utterly bewildering and incomprehensible to a majority of shareholders. Wall Street tended to blame the Administration and (paradoxically enough, in view of its support of U. S. steel a month before) argued that Washington should intervene to stimulate both the market and the economy. Administration officials argued that the market was overdue for a correction and insisted that the economy was sound. During the first week of June the market continued to decline, and President Kennedy, responding to the widespread demand that he take action, outlined a moderate program for stimulating the economy. It consisted of a plea for action by Congress on the variety of measures already before it (the tax credit on new investment in machinery and equipment, for example) and a promise of a tax cut in 1963. To many of his critics, however, the President was too late with too little.

The spanking which the President gave the steel executives, combined with the precipitate drop in stock prices, created among American businessmen, as we have said, a pervasive distrust of the Administration. Not since the 1930's when the business community bitterly assailed Franklin Roosevelt had an American President been subject to such abuse by the leaders of business and finance. Kennedy was pictured as an irresponsible socialist, a would-be dictator, and a visionary controlled by daffy left-wing professors. The President valiantly attempted to handle this crisis of confidence by reassuring business of the essential conservatism of his program. Speaking at the Yale commencement in June, for example, the President argued that cooperation between business and government was not only desirable but essential and could be achieved by breaking with outmoded habits of thought. But the business community apparently demanded more than words to convince them of the good will of the Administration.

Fortunately for the President, however, this business animus had little influence on congressional debate on the single most important legislative issue of the 87th Congress—the Administration's trade bill.

The chief aim of his trade program, the President emphasized, was to prepare the United States for adjustment

to vast changes in world conditions. The most dramatic
of these changes was the growth and prosperity of the

"Don't You Know This Is the Space Age?"

Basset
in *The Honolulu Star-Bulletin*

European Common Market consisting of France, West
Germany, Italy, the Netherlands, Belgium, and Luxembourg. Great Britain was seeking admission to the Market

73

and other European nations wished a close association with it. The economic uncertainties in the United States were in striking contrast to the economic confidence in Continental Europe. There, under the impetus of the Common Market, business was booming—production was up 40% since 1955, trade was up 58%. Economic growth in Western European countries, moreover, was at a faster rate than in the United States; while our growth had averaged only 3% annually, the annual increases in Germany and Italy, for example, had been 7.5% and 5.8% respectively. If Great Britain should gain admittance to the Common Market (and it appeared certain during the early months of the year that she would), a vast supernational economic system would be created which, in time, would rival the industrial might of the United States. From the American standpoint the rivalry was welcomed, for after all a united and prosperous Europe had been a basic goal of American foreign policy since the inauguration of the Marshall Plan in 1948. But the creation of an extensive and prosperous free-trade area and the erection of a common tariff to keep out outsiders did require a revaluation of American trade policy.

The President's answer to the challenge of the Common Market was his Trade Expansion Act, a measure which he termed a "bold new instrument of American trade policy." Under this plan he could eliminate altogether the tariffs on items in which the United States and the Common Market together do most of the world's business, and could cut other tariffs up to 50% over five years.

The "wholly new trade instrument" for which the President called was the most striking departure in United States policy on foreign trade since 1934 when Congress gave Franklin D. Roosevelt authority to lower the record-high Smoot-Hawley tariffs by as much as one-half. Such a new departure obviously would not be made without strenuous opposition. Protectionists argued (and many Congressmen were impressed by the argument) that to encourage the sale of imported goods in the United States would decrease the domestic demand for American goods. Many business and union leaders therefore demanded more, not less, tariff protection. But after months of hearings and thousands of complaints, the Congress chose to promote national advantage even at the expense of some individual hardship.

The passage of President Kennedy's bill early in July by an overwhelming margin in the House (it passed the Senate in September by a similarly large vote) prevented the year's congressional session from becoming an utter disaster for the Administration. The trade bill, which gave President Kennedy more sweeping power to reduce tariffs than any other President ever had, was his most substantial accomplishment in Congress. It gave him the unprecedented grant of new tariff-cutting powers that he had sought, and provided at the same time a program of "trade adjustment assistance" to American businessmen and workers injured by increased imports of competitive products. The Administration's triumph was marred by only one minor defeat—it failed to block a proviso which prohibited the Administration from granting any trade concessions to Poland or Yugoslavia.

If the success of the Common Market prompted a new departure in legislation on American foreign trade, the threat which the Market presented to the continued sale of American farm surplus in Europe focused attention on the domestic farm problem. That problem has been constant throughout the postwar era. Its roots are expanding agricultural output made possible by accelerating technological advance which has steadily increased the amount grown on each acre of farm land. Its harvest is a vast surplus and steadily climbing government expenditures to support crop prices and to halt the decline in farm incomes.

President Kennedy's farm program in 1962 was based on the same premise as the proposals which he made in 1961 and which never even advanced to the stage of being debated. Both were based on the argument that the government must deal with the farm surplus by imposing strict controls on production. The plans of the two years differed, however, in the techniques proposed to accomplish this goal.

Congressional debate on Kennedy's program demonstrated again, as it annually has done for a decade or more, the political sacredness of the farm vote. The bitter debate on the farm bill centered on whether the measure would open the door to regimentation of farmers by Federal fiat (a curious argument in view of the socialization of agriculture some two-and-a-half decades ago), with Republicans arguing that the bill would make Secretary of Agriculture Orville L. Freeman a czar. The bill was finally defeated by Republicans and disaffected Democrats. President Kennedy had to settle for a substitute bill extending for a year the existing voluntary control program, with provisions for mandatory production curbs applying the following year to wheat alone.

By the time the Congress gave the Administration a substitute and unsatisfactory farm bill, the session was far advanced. The other pieces of "must" legislation—medicare and aid to education—proposed by the Administration early in the session already had been defeated. The President's modest proposal to increase the Social Security tax by $\frac{1}{2}$ of 1% to finance hospital care for citizens over 65 years old appeared to shock many Congressmen who professed to see it as a giant step on the dreaded road to socialism. Most older voters and many other people only found it shocking that Congress was willing to appropriate billions for defense and not one cent for the needy. To still other people, congressional shock seemed less genuine than contrived by the well-financed lobby of the American Medical Association. The refusal of the President's request for $5.7 billion to be spent on aid to the nation's schools and colleges in the next five years was primarily due to the familiar congressional dispute over whether to include aid to parochial schools. It was also due, strangely enough, to the opposition of the influential

National Education Association, an organization which presumably would benefit by an enlarged Federal program of aid to education. The officers of the Association sent telegrams to all House members protesting that part of the bill which would provide grants for constructing libraries and science and engineering buildings in public and private colleges alike. Such a measure, it was contended, "imperils America's traditional concept of separation of church and state."

On civil rights, one of the most urgent domestic problems of our time, the President did not propose nor did Congress volunteer any major reform program. The Kennedy Administration did support a bill providing that a sixth-grade education should be adequate proof of literacy for a vote in Federal elections, a measure which was designed to prevent Southern Negroes from being disfranchised by arbitrary tests of literacy. But the skillful attempt of Senate Majority Leader Mike Mansfield to obviate a Southern filibuster by parliamentary maneuvers was no match for Southern determination to kill the bill. On the other hand, Southerners did allow, after a token ten-day filibuster, the passage of a constitutional amendment to outlaw the poll tax as a qualification for voting in elections for Federal office. This cooperativeness, however, demonstrated no conversion to the cause of Negro rights; it rather suggested that the poll tax (retained in only five states) is no longer so important as are other barriers to Negro voting in the South.

One's estimate of the progress made in the South during recent years depends on the criteria by which progress is assessed. If, for example, one measures the progress in the desegregation of Southern schools since 1954 against the more than two-century long history of segregation, he agrees with Southern moderates that great progress has been made during the last eight years. If, on the other hand, he assesses the rate of desegregation since 1954 in terms of the speed which is necessary to make up for centuries of injustice, he agrees with those Negro leaders who argue that the rate is far too slow. Moderate reformers could point to the fact that as of August, 1962 (according to the *Southern School News*), 948 out of 3047 Southern school districts had abandoned the color bar. More radical reformers could point out in rebuttal that those Southern states (such as North Carolina and Virginia) which allegedly have complied with the Supreme Court's rulings on desegregation have adopted only token integration, and that in Alabama, South Carolina, and Mississippi not a single school district has tried even token integration. As with desegregation, so with voting rights and other civil rights. Token gestures have been made but no wholesale reforms attempted.

Whether a moderate or a radical on the race issue, one could only applaud the defeat suffered by the die-hard segregationists of Mississippi in the year 1962. The registration of the first Negro at the University of Mississippi was not only a milestone in the history of desegregation, but a vindication of a basic American constitutional principle—the idea that our government is one of laws and not of men. It represented the triumph of the concept of orderly constitutional government over the view, presumably discredited by the Civil War, that a minority can violate with impunity the laws of the nation or interpret for itself the nature of the Union. In the long story of Federal-state relations, the story of James H. Meredith is an important paragraph.

A Federal court had ordered that Meredith be admitted to the University of Mississippi at the beginning of the college term in the fall of 1962. In other Southern states Negroes had been admitted to universities under similar court orders and in the face of local public hostility. But in Mississippi, as the editor of the *Atlanta Constitution* remarked, the newspapers, the politicians, the clergy, and the businessmen—in short, the power structure of the state—were dedicated to total defiance. In other Southern states the Supreme Court's school decision was regarded as a mistake. In Mississippi it was interpreted as a Communist plot. In most other Southern states there were moderates and liberals willing to speak out against the extremists of the White Citizens Council. In Mississippi, such rational men, if they existed, were wholly silent.

Mr. Meredith's enrollment at the 114-year-old University of Mississippi was the climax of a week of conflict between state officials and Federal marshals. Meredith, accompanied by James P. McShane, Chief U. S. Marshal, and John Doar, first assistant in the Justice Department's Civil Rights Division, repeatedly presented himself at the University for registration in compliance with the Court's order. His registration was repeatedly blocked, first by Gov. Ross R. Barnett backed up by a group of Mississippi legislators, then by Lt. Gov. Paul B. Johnson backed up by highway patrolmen. In the meantime, a Federal Court of Appeals found Gov. Barnett and Lt. Gov. Johnson guilty of contempt of court, and ruled that continued defiance of the Court would result in a heavy fine. But the Mississippi executives refused even to accept the service of the citation. The officials of Mississippi with the power of the state behind them were determined to resist the enrollment of James Meredith by violence and bloodshed if necessary; Justice Department officials, with the superior power of the Federal government behind them, were just as determined to carry out the orders of the Federal Court. A showdown was inevitable and its outcome certain.

On the night of September 30, Meredith, accompanied by Federal marshals, entered the University. His admission was made possible by Gov. Barnett's assurances to President Kennedy that the state would not block the attempt, and by the President's conclusion that he could trust Barnett. But whatever Barnett's assurances (and there was disagreement on the facts), the President's trust was misplaced. Meredith's arrival on the campus touched off a night of rioting.

The bloody night of September 30, 1962, was one of those stains on our national honor which time will not easily erase. Because one lone Negro was on the campus and wished to be admitted to the University of Missis-

81

sippi, a crowd of 2,500 students and "hoodlums," in Robert F. Kennedy's phrase, used bricks, lead pipes and shot guns in an assault on Federal officials. Did Mississippians repent this riot that took two lives and left approximately 375 injured? To die-hard segregationists— and most Mississippians can be so classified—the unhappy affair at Oxford was all due to the tyrannical Kennedys and to an authoritarian national state. They remained as sullenly defiant of Federal authority as before. The extremists' position was stated by Charles M. Hills, writing in the *Clarion Ledger* of Jackson, Mississippi. He warned that "the scalawags and the moderates are going to crawl out of the walls now." "Watch the peace-lovers come to the fore, grab a nigger-neck and start bellowing brotherly love," he continued. "For us . . . we'll just go on being a bigot, a reactionary, a rebel and lick our wounds till the next fight starts and plan to win somehow. We are licked but not beaten."

Some 10,000 Army troops and federalized National Guardsmen were necessary to restore order in Oxford, and deputy U. S. marshals were necessary to protect Meredith against possible attacks by his fellow students and outraged townspeople. James Meredith remained at the University of Mississippi for the remaining months of 1962. The wall of segregation in Mississippi had been scaled. But it was scarcely reassuring to know that it had taken the U. S. Army to get Meredith inside the white compound and a bodyguard of Federal marshals to keep him there. For Meredith personally, his victory must have been a hollow one indeed; to Gov. Ross Barnett and his supporters, defeat was believed to be only temporary; but to most Americans, an important principle had been maintained—the principle that Americans who disagree with the law shall not be allowed to disobey it.

Meanwhile, the congressional session dragged on into the autumn. As Labor Day, the original target for adjournment, passed, many Congressmen appeared to be increasingly restive, a symptom which was diagnosed by journalistic physicians as election fever. By early October, there was all the haste and frantic quarreling that usually mark the approaching end of a Congress, and finally on October 13 the 87th Congress adjourned. What, in summary, could be said of its record? What did its history reveal about the leadership of President Kennedy? To both questions the best answer is a negative one; it was not so much what was done as what was left undone that disturbed many Americans.

Shortly before the adjournment, Kennedy asserted that no Congress in American history had done so much for the people as the 87th. Yet a good many Americans believed that Congress should have been willing to do far more than it did. Liberals asked if it was too much to expect the richest country in the world to educate its children properly and to care for its aged. Thoughtful city dwellers asked if it was consistent to spend billions of dollars annually to subsidize farmers while refusing even to admit the seriousness of urban problems by creating a cabinet position for their representative. Negroes asked if it was not time to demand that Congress energetically try to blot from the national escutcheon the stain of racial bigotry by guaranteeing to Negroes, at once and effectively, the right to full equality with their white fellow citizens in school, in employment, in housing, in travel, in voting. Finally, many thoughtful Americans asked if the President had provided the dynamic, crusading leadership in domestic affairs of which he presumably is capable. President Kennedy should have used his immense popularity, they argued, to persuade the American people to support bold and progressive policies.

President Kennedy's record as well as that of the Congress was at issue in the mid-term elections of 1962. But given the President's enormous popularity (according to Mr. Gallup's stethoscope some 70% of the American people approved of the manner in which he was doing his job) and his apparent preference for the middle of the road, it was not easy for the Republicans to discover issues on which they might ride into office in November. Many businessmen were dissatisfied, as we have seen, with what they considered the President's attempt to push the steel companies around; most physicians were angry with the Administration for the medicare program it proposed; many Southerners were disgruntled at the Federal government's advocacy of fairer treatment for American Negroes; conservative Republicans were adamantly opposed to the President's promotion of what they considered a socialistic program; the John Birchers of the far right persisted in their bizarre conviction that many prominent officials in Washington were agents of international communism. These groups could be expected to oppose the Administration whatever tack the campaign might take. What was needed was an issue which would rally the support of moderate Republicans and independent Democrats. Cuba, it was soon discovered, might be such an issue.

By August it was common knowledge that the Soviets were engaged in a large-scale military build-up in Cuba. For at least two years the United States had been gravely concerned by the steady strengthening of the economic ties between Moscow and Havana. The sending of Soviet arms and troops to Cuba greatly heightened American anxiety.

Throughout the summer and early fall the Administration was under heavy pressure to launch an invasion of Cuba, to impose a blockade, or to take any one of a number of suggested actions to topple Castro and remove a bothersome and noisome neighbor. Strangely enough, sentiment for the invasion of Cuba appeared to be strongest in the Midwest, the section in which isolationism traditionally has been strongest. This jingoism was owing to many factors—to impatience with a stalemated cold war which promised to last for a generation to come; irritation that the United States should be confronted with a Communist regime on its front doorstep; vestigial remains of the attitude of a generation or so ago that Cuba is a protectorate of the United States; the belief that the Cuban crisis was a convenient stick with which to beat the Democrats. But this jingoism was more than offset by the caution of a large number of Americans who feared that direct action, in view of Russia's deep commitment to the Castro regime, might lead to an atomic war or, at the least, might alienate Latin Americans, traditionally wary of United States power in the hemisphere.

In an attempt to steer a course between the extremes of bellicosity and timidity, the Kennedy Administration tried to meet the Cuban challenge with political and economic measures. On the one hand, an effort was made to solidify hemispheric isolation of Cuba; on the other, Europeans were urged to cease supplying Cuba with the sinews of war. Many Latin Americans, however, opposed new restrictions against Cuba, and non-Communist shippers were reluctant to drop the lucrative Cuban trade.

As Soviet arms and men piled up in Cuba, the public clamor for President Kennedy to "do something," no matter what the consequences, increased in volume. Kennedy, however, continued to handle the problem circumspectly. Early in September he said that there was no "evidence of . . . significant offensive capability" in Cuba, but he added that "were it to be otherwise the gravest issues would arise. . . ." Republican Congressmen, perhaps in search of a campaign issue, were more responsive to the popular mood than was the President and proposed to give the President authority to use troops for an invasion of Cuba, an authorization which he presumably did not wish for an invasion he did not wish to launch. The President's political counterstroke was to ask Congress for standby authority to call up military reserves in case of need. On September 26 Congress adopted a resolution which was a compromise between the Republican proposal and the President's request. Kennedy, however, chose to interpret it as a demand for action if, and only if, the Cubans threatened violence to the rest of the hemisphere. This interpretation was plainly not what the majority of Congressmen or the majority of people who wrote them letters really wanted. What they wanted, in the words of one publicist, was "to shave Dr. Castro with a blunt razor."

Premier Khrushchev provided Kennedy a way out of the Cuban dilemma, but in so doing imperiled the peace of the world. When President Kennedy accepted the daredevil challenge of the Russians over Cuba, the nightmare of nuclear destruction, which has disturbed the earth's repose since the destruction of Hiroshima in 1945, briefly appeared an imminent reality.

By mid-October seasoned Washington reporters sensed an unusual tenseness in the Capital's political air and guessed that an international crisis of major proportions was brewing. By October 21, a Sunday, the tenseness increased. Important presidential aides came to the White House; urgent meetings were underway at the State and Defense Departments and the Central Intelligence Agency; congressional leaders were asked to return to Washington. The meaning of all this activity was shrouded in secrecy. On the afternoon of October 21 it was announced that the President would go on television in the evening with a message of great "national emergency." At 7 P.M. the well-kept secret was told.

The crisis, President Kennedy explained to an anxious nation, concerned Cuba. "Within the past week," he said, "unmistakable evidence has established the fact that a series of offensive missile sites is now in preparation on that imprisoned island." What would the United States do about it? The President replied that "to halt this offensive build-up a strict quarantine of all offensive military equipment under shipment to Cuba is being initiated. . . ." The President did not say that the United States was imposing a "blockade," for under international law a blockade is an act of war. Whatever niceties of language might be used, however, it was obvious that the United States was doing so, for the Navy was directed to order ships carrying offensive weapons to Cuba to turn back or to face sinking. The "quarantine," Kennedy emphasized, would not be lifted until the Administration was assured that the missiles had been withdrawn and the bases dismantled. On whom would the blame be placed for the military build-up, on whom the responsibility for maintaining the peace, Cuba or Russia? ". . . it shall be the policy of this nation," Kennedy said, "to regard any nuclear missile launched from Cuba against any nation in the Western Hemisphere as an attack by the Soviet Union on the United States requiring a full retaliatory response on the Soviet Union." The President announced, ominously, that he had ordered stepped-up surveillance of

Wide World Photos

Chief Justice Earl Warren administers presidential oath of office to John F. Kennedy, January 20, 1961. Lyndon B. Johnson, incoming Vice-President, is at right; former President Eisenhower stands at left.

Robert Frost reading one of his poems at President Kennedy's inauguration.

United Press International Photo

President Kennedy and Mrs. Kennedy with President Charles de Gaulle and his wife at the theater in Versailles on the occasion of the Kennedys' visit to France in June, 1961.

Royal Laotian troops board helicopter supplied by tl United States as part of tl program of American milita advisory assistance to the an communist fighters.

Astronaut Alan B. Shepard, Jr. on his way to make the first rocket flight into space by a United States flier—May 5, 1961—from Cape Canaveral, Florida.

Virgil Grissom enters space capsule for the second rocket flight launched from Cape Canaveral, July 21.

Wide World Photos

Boating—a new popular sport

Courtesy, Evinrude Motors, Milwaukee, Wisc.

Courtesy, Kroch's and Brentano's, Chicago, Ill.

Readers browsing in the paperback section of a large bookstore

Marine Lt. Colonel John H. Glenn as he arrived aboard the carrier U.S.S. *Randolph,* February 20, 1962, following his three-orbit flight in *Friendship 7.*

Navy Lt. Commander M. Scott Carpenter just before entry into the space capsule *Aurora* at Cape Canaveral, Florida, May 24, for his orbital flight.

President Kennedy with Navy Commander Walter M. Schirra, Jr., and his family after the astronaut's six-orbit flight.

Aerial view of a missile base in Cuba. The various sections of the base are labeled.

President Kennedy and Mrs. Kennedy with their guests at a White House musicale at which Isaac Stern, violinist, played.

The auditorium of the new Philharmonic Hall, first building to be completed in the Lincoln Center for Performing Arts in New York City.

William Faulkner, Nobel
Prize novelist, who died at
the age of 64.

Photo by Ralph Thompson.
Courtesy of Random House.

Photo by KARSH, Ottawa.
Courtesy of Harper and Row.

Mrs. Eleanor Roosevelt, wife of
the late President F. D. Roosevelt, author and UN representative, whose death inspired many
tributes from all over the world.
She was known as the "First Lady
of the World."

United Press International Photo

John Steinbeck, American novelist, receives the
Nobel Prize from King Gustaf Adolf in Stockholm.

President John F. Kennedy at a news conference

United States Secretary of State Dean Rusk, Soviet Foreign Minister Andrei Gromyko and British Foreign Secretary Lord Home sign the nuclear test ban treaty in Moscow.

The March on behalf of Civil Rights, Washington, August 28, 1963

Henry Cabot Lodge received by South Viet Nam's President Ngo Dinh Diem, after presenting his credentials as U. S. Ambassador

Peace Corps Volunteer Barbara J. Wylie, of Ypsilanti, Michigan, is an English teacher in Nepal. She has also started a school for the children of "untouchable" servants.

Courtesy Peace Corps

Peace Corps Volunteer Willie Douglas of Tampa, Florida, teaches agricultural science at a rural "pilot high school" in northwest Pakistan.

Courtesy Peace Corps

Lyndon B. Johnson is sworn in as President of the United States November 22, 1963, in the cabin of the presidential plane; Mrs. John F. Kennedy stands at his side.

Wide World Photos

Wide World Photos

World leaders walk in President Kennedy's funeral procession on November 25 as it leaves the White House. *From left, front row,* Heinrich Lubke, West German President; French President Charles de Gaulle; Queen Frederika of Greece; King Baudouin of Belgium; Emperor Haile Selassie of Ethiopia; and President Diosdado Macapagal of the Philippines.

Cuba and had directed the armed forces "to prepare for any eventualities."

The Russian bluff, if it was that, had been called; the alleged view in the Kremlin that the United States, like all liberal nations, lacks the will to fight had been boldly refuted; Castro's attempt to deal with the United States from behind a wall of Soviet nuclear strength had been thwarted. In accomplishing these things President Kennedy had pushed the world to the brink of an atomic holocaust. A shove from Khrushchev, and its precarious toe hold would be lost. What would Russia do? Fear mounted as it was reported that the armed forces of the Soviet and other Warsaw Pact nations had been alerted. Was 1962 to be another 1914? It was remembered by those conscious of history that in 1914 the mobilization of the great powers, once started, carried Europe inexorably, and perhaps unnecessarily, to war.

On Wednesday, October 24, the world breathed a collective sigh of relief: the deadline for the imposition of the "quarantine" came and passed without incident. Russian ships which were approaching Cuba changed course, indicating Russia's unwillingness to face an immediate showdown. Even more encouraging, Soviet Premier Khrushchev, in a letter to British pacifist Lord Bertrand Russell, castigated the United States but also suggested a summit meeting to avert war. Khrushchev presumably realized that he must withdraw, as gracefully as possible, from the predicament in which his rash behavior had put him.

On October 28, one week after President Kennedy's television message, Khrushchev formally capitulated. In a message to Kennedy the Russian Premier said the Soviet missiles in Cuba would be dismantled and shipped back to Russia under UN supervision and asked that the United States, in turn, commit itself not to invade Cuba. Kennedy, playing the role of magnanimous victor as ably as Khrushchev shrewdly played the role of peacemaker, congratulated Khrushchev on his "statesmanlike decision" and agreed to this *quid pro quo*. He made it clear, however, that withdrawing of the quarantine and the pledge not to invade Cuba hinged on "effective international verification" of the removal of the offensive weapons and the cessation of any additional missile shipments to Cuba. Despite a number of diplomatic loose ends that remained to be tied, the Cuban crisis appeared to be all but over by the end of November. The chief stumbling block to a definite conclusion was Premier Castro. His prestige badly damaged by the obvious demonstration that Russia calls the tune to which he capers, Castro attempted to salve his wounded pride by refusing to accept any form of UN inspection. Castro's stubbornness gave the United States a good reason to continue its reconnaissance flights and, perhaps, to modify its pledge not to invade Cuba.

It was in the afterglow of President Kennedy's victory over Premier Khrushchev that the mid-term elections of 1962 took place. It would be absurd to charge, as a few rabid partisans hinted, that the Kennedy Administration had promoted the Cuban crisis to win the election, but the Democratic party was certainly the beneficiary of President Kennedy's bold defiance of the Russians. Just as the Suez crisis of October and November, 1956, had rallied the American people behind President Eisenhower and destroyed whatever chances of victory Adlai Stevenson may have had to win the presidency, so the Cuban crisis rallied the electorate behind Kennedy and the Democrats. The Democrats picked up four Senate seats, bringing their already wide margin to 68–32, the largest margin since the Roosevelt landslide in 1936. In the House battle they fought the Republicans to a standstill—the line-up in the 88th Congress would be 258–177, as compared with 258–174 in the 87th Congress. Despite predictions that the Republicans would win a large number of gubernatorial seats held by Democrats, the Democrats managed to hold their own. The G.O.P. did, however, unseat Democratic Governors in three major states—Pennsylvania, Ohio and Michigan.

The Democratic victory was the more impressive when one remembers that only once since the Civil War (in 1934) has the President's party gained congressional strength in a mid-term election. But what did the Democratic victory mean? The electorate obviously favored the containment of communism and heartily applauded the President's stern rebuke to Premier Khrushchev and Fidel Castro. What else it favored was not so certain.

The 51,000,000 Americans who went to the polls on November 6 probably only reaffirmed the well-known political fact that in the midst of an economic boom the voters seldom react strongly to domestic issues. And in November, 1962, the economy was booming. The rate of economic growth was still lagging; the large number of unemployed continued to suggest a fundamental disorder underneath the country's apparent economic health. But profits and wages were high, the stock market was booming, and most Americans were more interested in buying the mounds of goods displayed by stores in anticipation of Christmas than in thinking about nettlesome subjects such as the international balance of trade or the rate of our economic growth.

Although the Administration and the public, as has been said, were freer in 1962 than in previous years to concentrate on domestic affairs, foreign affairs continued to demand a large portion of the energy and time of our national leaders. They also continued to be of major personal concern to all Americans, if only because the existence of terrifyingly destructive weapons of war coupled with easily ignitible international tensions create the ever constant possibility of nuclear annihilation.

The major international problem which confronted the United States in the year 1962 was the same problem it had wrestled with since World War II—the containment of communism. In 1962, as in previous years, the contest between Russia and the United States was global. It centered first in one area, then in another—at the traffic checkpoints of West Berlin, in the jungles of Southeast Asia, in the forum of the United Nations, in the heart of

Africa, in the Middle East, in South America, and even in the atmosphere above the nuclear testing grounds.

What was the situation in these areas at the beginning of the year? What had been done by the year's end to attenuate the problems which confronted us in each? In the strife-torn Congo, eighteen perilous months of independence and all the efforts of the UN had not resulted in a viable federal government; instead, the bitter dispute between the Congolese central government and the secessionist province of Katanga which had hamstrung the UN operation from the beginning continued to frustrate it. In Southeast Asia, Communist aggression in Laos and South Vietnam continued to pose serious obstacles to the attempt of the United States to save that region from communism. In Europe, Premier Khrushchev continued to press for recognition of the East German regime by the Western powers and, to this end, continued his harassments in West Berlin. Also in Europe, negotiations between Great Britain and the Common Market continued, and on their outcome the future of our Atlantic Alliance depended. In the United Nations, the continued domination of the Assembly by an Afro-Asian majority made that organization (in the view of many Americans) a weak and precarious foundation for American foreign policy.

More important perhaps than any one of these difficulties was the overriding problem of the control of nuclear weapons. After seventeen years of talks, East-West disarmament negotiations remained stalemated. The one positive achievement of this long period had been a three-year moratorium on testing which began in 1958. But on September 1, 1961, the Russians broke the moratorium and subsequently conducted between forty and fifty nuclear tests, including one bomb of more than fifty megatons. As the Russians, obviously indifferent to world opinion or health, conducted test after test, an intense debate began in the United States on whether to resume atmospheric testing.

Another disarmament conference, to be attended by eighteen nations, was scheduled to meet in Geneva on March 14, 1962. In view of the dismal record of past conferences, few people were so optimistic as to predict any resolution of the different approaches to disarmament advocated by East and West (the West repeatedly has demanded controls that would prevent violations of a test ban; Russia consistently has refused to agree to the safeguards the West considers essential). But the presence of a new factor in the negotiations allowed at least a flicker of hope. The new factor was President Kennedy's decision to resume atmospheric tests in April unless the Soviet Union agreed to accept a test ban treaty. As the possibility of another failure at Geneva became apparent and with it United States resumption of nuclear tests a certainty, Premier Khrushchev began to play his favorite game of summitry. But the Western nations, aware that he was engaging primarily in a propaganda exercise, refused to participate.

The conference which assembled in Geneva on March

14, 1962, had been eighteen months in the making (it took two UN General Assembly debates before agreement could even be reached on which nations would participate), but it was only a few weeks in demonstrating that it would go the way of its predecessors. The work of the conference was accurately summed up by the Soviet delegate who said: "There is complete stalemate—no advance of any kind, no change of positions." Both sides had gone to Geneva prepared to make "new look" proposals, but, once there, neither side was willing to do anything about the fundamental issue which has obviated progress in arms limitations since World War II—the mutual suspicion, fear, insecurity, and mistrust which makes each side believe that the other does not wish to achieve any major disarmament. The negotiations dragged fitfully on through the late spring and summer. Early in September the weary delegates recessed and happily turned the debate over to the United Nations, scheduled to meet on September 18.

After the failure of the Geneva conference, the United States went ahead with its plans for the resumption of tests. By April 21, a task force of 12,000 men and 100 ships stood ready in the Pacific test area. As zero hour approached, demonstrations against the prospective tests were staged in many cities—15,000 marchers in London, a Quaker vigil in New York, and nineteen rallies in West Germany. Urgent personal appeals to cancel the tests were sent to President Kennedy; among them were pleas from U Thant, acting Secretary General of the United

Nations, and Prime Minister Nehru of India. But the President's decision was inflexible. On April 25 the Atomic Energy Commission issued a terse statement that a nuclear detonation had taken place over Britain's Christmas Island in the South Pacific. Two days later there was another atmospheric test in the Pacific and an underground test in Nevada.

Despite Moscow's barrage of invective, the diplomatic and propaganda fallout from the Pacific explosion was surprisingly slight. There were of course demonstrations and protests in a number of neutral countries, but there appeared to be an awareness among some of the neutrals that Russia bore much of the responsibility for having broken the moratorium, and that President Kennedy had been confronted with an extremely difficult decision. Both the United States and Russia conducted additional tests during the year. What military and scientific lessons they learned were of course shrouded in secrecy. The concerned layman could only doubt that any lesson learned by risking the health of millions yet to be born could be worthwhile. He furthermore could only be saddened by the reflection that the tests may have done no more than maintain a stalemate of terror.

Perhaps "stalemate," as has been suggested, is the term which most accurately describes Soviet-U. S. relations in the year 1962. In Germany, for example, the Soviets continued to press their demand that West Berlin be made a demilitarized "free city" and that East Germany be given control of its access routes. To further this goal, the Russians resorted to a variety of harassments; they restricted access by allied officials to East Berlin, and ordered Soviet planes to fly in the air corridors from West Germany to Berlin, among other things. But the Western nations stood firmly by their commitment to safeguard the freedom of Berlin and Khrushchev presumably did not wish to risk a war to achieve his goals.

Neither was the Russian Premier prepared to assume a bellicose stance in Southeast Asia. In Laos, Russia and the United States cooperated in an effort to install a neutralist regime. The United States sought a neutral status for Laos in the hope that it would prevent either a Communist take-over or a direct clash involving the big powers. The Soviet Union presumably did so to thwart the expansion of the influence of the Chinese Communists in that area and, like the United States, to avoid the involvement of the big powers at a time when international tensions were comparatively relaxed.

The agreement to establish a neutralist coalition regime in Laos was made by Premier Khrushchev and President Kennedy at their meeting in Vienna in June, 1961. Motivated by a desire to create a buffer zone between the Communist and Western power blocs, the two leaders supported the work of a fourteen-nation conference on Laos, set up under the co-chairmanship of Britain and Russia. The effort to bring peace to this strife-torn country, however, was complicated by bitterness and suspicion among the three Laotian factions—the pro-Western government led by Prince Boun Oum, the neutralists led by Prince Souvanna Phouma, and the pro-Communist Pathet Lao led by Prince Souphanouvong. Finally, in July, 1962, after two years of civil war and political wrangling, a neutralist coalition regime was installed. Had its tenure depended on the United States and Russia, there might have been reasonable hopes for its success. But the fact that it also depended on the Chinese Communists and their allies, the Communists in North Vietnam, cast grave doubts on its permanence. The remark made by the Chinese Foreign Minister just before the installation of the new regime was ominous: "Peace in Laos," he said, "cannot be regarded as consolidated so long as the flames of war are kept alive in South Vietnam."

The Chinese diplomat was referring to the bitter conflict in South Vietnam between Communist guerrillas, called Viet Cong, and the U. S. supported government of President Ngo Dinh Diem. During 1960-61, the Viet Cong gradually built up their strength in South Vietnam by means of an intensive campaign of threats and blandishments, ambush and murder. Their repeated victories threatened to destroy the last Western foothold in the great land mass of Southeast Asia and jeopardized the security not only of India but of United States allies in the Western Pacific. To prevent a Communist victory, the United States late in 1961 rushed aid to the South Vietnamese. Huge cargo planes brought in vast amounts of military equipment; transport planes brought in United States airmen and other military men to train the

South Vietnam army in the use of modern weapons and techniques.

During 1962 the United States operation in South Vietnam steadily expanded. In February the United States military mission there numbered about 4,000; by April it had increased to about 6,000, and by June to about 7,000. The Americans, it was obvious, were playing an increasingly important part in the struggle; they were training the Vietnamese army, flying the helicopters and light planes that carried Vietnamese soldiers into battle, and, acting on the President's orders, were firing back at the Communists if shot at. As United States aid increased, the Chinese Communists charged the United States with fighting an "undeclared war," and Americans asked with increasing urgency whether the United States was heading toward direct involvement in South Vietnam's war against the elusive Viet Cong guerrilla force.

It was not yet an American war, but it appeared likely that President Kennedy might soon be confronted with the painful dilemma of making it one, or of witnessing the loss of South Vietnam to communism or, perhaps, of helping in the creation of a neutralist government which, as had happened in Laos, might allow us to withdraw gracefully from a commitment too risky to be honored.

Just as the prestige of the United States was heavily involved in Southeast Asia, so it was also at stake in Africa. But the situation confronting the United States in these two areas was different and demanded different solutions. In South Vietnam the United States committed its own troops and money to prop up the weak regime of President Diem; in the Congo its efforts to strengthen the government of Premier Cyrille Adoula were undertaken under the aegis of the United Nations. In South Vietnam there was a clash with well-armed Communist guerrillas; in the Congo there was a dispute with the well-financed Katanga government of Moise Tshombe. In South Vietnam there was a conflict, although indirect, with Communist China; in the Congo operation there were differences, however muted, with our Western allies.

The UN operation in the Congo was stymied in 1962, as in 1961, by the problem which had hindered its success from the beginning—ending the secession of Katanga province, the source of half the Congo's wealth. Without Katanga the Congo has little hope of becoming a successful nation. The *Union Minière du Haut-Katanga,* controlled by Belgium and, to a lesser extent, British interests, exports $240 million worth of copper, cobalt and other minerals annually and pays $40 million in taxes to the Katanga government. The rest of the Congo exports $37.5 million a year and is doomed to bankruptcy without a share of Katanga's revenues. Just by sitting still, therefore, Tshombe has been undermining the central Congolese government in Leopoldville. What could the United Nations do? Its Congo operation, costing $10 million monthly, was threatening it with bankruptcy; some solution to the Congo chaos was imperative.

Early in the fall U Thant, the United Nations' Acting Secretary General, offered a plan for federating the

Congo. It called for a reunion of the Katanga and Congolese armies and for a sharing of Katanga's mining revenues with Leopoldville on a 50-50 basis. Should Tshombe continue to stall, the UN plan recommended the use of economic sanctions. Twice within fifteen months (in September and December, 1961) the United Nations had used arms against the soldiers of Katanga to force Tshombe to join the Congo. Each time the wily President had made promises which he later skillfully evaded. If force could not persuade him, could economic persuasion do so? The answer was given late in December when United Nations forces found themselves for the third time involved in military action against Katanga. According to U Thant's account, UN soldiers were drawn into this action on December 28 by the persistent firing against them that had been kept up by the Katangans through the Christmas week. Ignoring the British demand for an immediate cease fire, the UN forces quickly seized control of much of Katanga. Tshombe announced in January, 1963, that it was all over. Had he capitulated? Given his record of slippery negotiating tactics, any predictions about the Congo are risky. But it appeared that the United Nations operation was decisive and that Tshombe at long last would be forced to join the Congo.

The UN action in the Congo received the unqualified support of the United States and only the lukewarm support of its Western allies, Britain, France, and Belgium. The British government, fearful of what the United Nations might do in Rhodesia and concerned over British financial interests in Katanga, gave the UN action only verbal support; the French, determined to retain their influence in their former colonies, favored Tshombe's separatism; most Belgians probably felt the same way, although the United States had persuaded the Belgian government to support its policies. But if the United States did not win the praise of its allies, it received the plaudits of the African and Asian nations who wish to see a financially sound and a strong Congo.

United States-allied differences over the Congo were symptomatic. A chief problem of the architects of American foreign policy in the year 1962 was a deepening rift in our Western alliance. The chief Western maverick was President Charles de Gaulle whose attempts to restore France to the prestige and grandeur she once enjoyed have led him to oppose United States plans for NATO and for Western Europe and to offer himself as the leader of a European community. Konrad Adenauer, Germany's aging Chancellor, appeared willing to play de Gaulle's game of follow the leader; other European nations were more reluctant.

What were the issues on which de Gaulle and the United States differed? De Gaulle ridiculed the Geneva disarmament conference, criticized the United States for resuming nuclear tests, and insisted that France would have to build its own nuclear deterrent and conduct its own tests. One reason for his determination on the latter score was his failure to get President Kennedy to share nuclear information with France. De Gaulle also insisted that the only possible form of European integration was his own project for a "Europe of States." He lampooned the ideas for supranationalism supported by the United States as "utopian structures" and "myths, stories, parades." On Berlin, de Gaulle scored the United States efforts to negotiate a settlement with the Russians. Berlin's status, he insisted, "should not be changed and we would not . . . accept a measure" altering any of the rights of the Western powers in Berlin.

De Gaulle's distant attitude toward the Atlantic Alliance, his independence and imperiousness, created a serious dilemma for the United States. A united and prosperous Europe had been a major goal of our foreign policy, as has been said, since the Marshall Plan of 1948. What should we do if we achieved our goal only to find ourselves confronted by a Europe intent on following a policy at odds with our own? Should we acquiesce, or should we remind our allies that he who pays the fiddler can call the tune? On the answer to this question, obviously, hung the future of the Western Alliance.

Just as the Marshall Plan had helped to create a strong and prosperous Europe, so it was hoped that the Latin American equivalent of that plan would bolster the tottering economies of our Southern neighbors. The Kennedy Administration's answer to the challenge of Latin America was the Alliance for Progress. Announced by the President in March, 1961, and ratified by the Latin American nations six months later, the Alliance for Progress is a ten-year multi-billion dollar plan whose purpose, in the words of its charter, is to bring to Latin Americans "accelerated economic progress and broader social justice within the framework of personal dignity and political liberty." The Alliance sets ambitious goals: six years of free schooling for all children, literacy for 50,000,000 people now illiterate, eradication of malaria, large-scale public housing, potable water for more than half the population. The act also pledges the Latin Americans to two basic, and controversial, reforms. One is agrarian reform, distributing large landholdings now in the hands of a small minority. The other is tax reform, redistributing the national income in order to benefit those who are most in need.

The accomplishments of the Alliance during its first year were impressive indeed. By the spring of 1962, five Latin American countries were pressing land reform, and, despite the shortage of trained economists, all the countries had accepted the concept of nation-wide development planning and had introduced central planning boards. More dramatic were the first concrete signs of the program's impact. For example, in the troubled Andean Department in Peru a school lunch program was inaugurated during the first months of the Alliance. About 26,000 children were fed by surplus U. S. food, and school attendance rose 50%. Finally, within the short space of one year, the Alliance had become the cornerstone of U. S. foreign policy in the hemisphere, dedicated to the proposition that Latin America must evolve peacefully and democratically toward social justice and prosperity and must not fall prey to violent revolutions that could result in Communist control.

Despite these accomplishments, no one predicts that the road to a better life for Latin America via the route of the Alliance for Progress will be straight or smooth. Some of the impediments are already apparent. For example, there are grave doubts among many North Americans whether the money committed to the Alliance is doing what it is supposed to do—that is, encourage the Latin American recipients to help themselves, especially by reforming their economic systems. There is also the question of how much reform the United States should demand before it provides aid. There is, finally, the problem of whether to grant aid to military strong men who seize control of Latin American countries and impose governments which are the antithesis of the type of democratic government the Alliance was designed to promote.

The last problem was one which beset the Kennedy Administration in 1962. In March, Argentina's military leaders threw out their duly elected president and imposed military rule. But the generals shrewdly preserved a coating of constitutional correctness by installing civilian figureheads. The United States, choosing not to probe behind the constitutional façade, continued its aid. Developments in Peru were more serious. On July 18, Peru's president was deposed and imprisoned because he refused to annul elections that had been won by a man the army disliked. Confronted by this undisguised contempt for

democratic institutions, the United States suspended diplomatic relations, held back the $81 million in Alliance
funds that had been allotted Peru, and cut off military
assistance. When the new regime responded by releas-
ing its political prisoners and by promising to hold and
respect free elections, the Kennedy Administration swal-
lowed its scruples and fears and recognized the new government. The Peruvian coup was, as President Kennedy
said, a setback; but the Administration concluded that to
withhold aid would have postponed urgently needed
amelioration of Peru's economic problems.

The year's difficulties in Argentina and Peru led some
critics of the Alliance Program to ask if Western democratic traditions could be expected to take root in countries
whose histories have not prepared them for it. The statesmen, North and South, who support the Alliance could
answer that a program so vast and so experimental neces-
sarily encounters mammoth difficulties. And they could
ask, in turn, if the goal of the Alliance—economic and
social improvements within a framework of democratic
institutions—was not splendid enough to permit a great
many setbacks.

Historians of the future may well stress aspects of the
American story in 1962 other than the political, economic,
and international developments which have dominated
this narrative. They may, for example, emphasize progress in the arts, or the record of scientific achievements,
or the state of American education, or the condition of
American literature. They may, again, be concerned with

the social record—with population changes, with subtle alterations in the structure of society and the family, or, more mundanely, with the events of the year which were highlighted in the tons of newsprint and thousands of magazines which rolled off American presses.

The scientific and technological changes of our time— in physics, chemistry, biology, medicine, geology, and engineering, for example—are so swift and often so complicated that few people can understand them and even fewer people keep abreast of them. The scientific revolution of the mid-20th century is perhaps more significant than that of the 17th century. But most educated men two centuries ago could understand the Newtonian universe; only a trained coterie can understand the universe of Einstein, Planck, and Van Allen. If one cannot understand, he can at least marvel, and the practical results of scientific research were fantastic enough to fire the imagination even of those least susceptible to enthusiasm.

The most spectacular of the year's many scientific achievements occurred in space. At the beginning of the year, the United States had launched 64 satellites and 33 remained in orbit; Russia (to make the inevitable comparison) had launched 15 and had 3 in orbit. But an American had yet to orbit the earth and thus enter the celestial olympics inaugurated by the Russian feats in 1961. Col. John H. Glenn became the first successful American contestant. Before dawn on February 20, Col. Glenn walked out to the launching pad at Cape Canaveral, Florida. As the sun rose, thousands watched the drama from the Canaveral beaches, and millions more throughout the country watched in front of television sets. The drama had a happy ending; the launching was successful, Glenn orbited the earth three times, and then made a happy landing.

After two days of intensive "de-briefing" and medical and other tests at Grand Turk Island near the Bahamas, Col. Glenn returned to Florida on Friday morning, February 23, escorted by Vice President Lyndon B. Johnson. More than 100,000 persons cheered him and swarmed around his car as he drove from the airport to Canaveral to meet President Kennedy. Two days later he was given a parade and huge public reception in Washington and addressed a joint session of Congress; from Washington he went to New York where the din of cheering, the blizzard of confetti, and the masses of people watching the parade up Broadway had Col. Glenn saying over and over again "Wow!" The American people had found a new hero and Glenn was made to order for the role.

Late in May, Comdr. Scott Carpenter followed Glenn into the stratosphere. His safe launching into space was taken almost for granted by the public; interest developed only with the movie scenario finale. For nearly an hour it was assumed that Comdr. Carpenter might be lost, or perhaps drowned, but he turned up safe and still filled with energy on a life raft in the Caribbean. On October 3, Comdr. Walter M. Schirra became the third astronaut to soar from Cape Canaveral; he returned to earth nine hours later after orbiting it six times, landing accurately in the Pacific beside the chief recovery ship. The continued success of the space trips removed a good deal of the glamour from the launchings; what was yesterday's fantastic speculation became today's prosaic fact. But they gave the American people a much-needed psychological lift and rendered more likely the ultimate success of the United States attempt to land three Americans on the moon before the end of the 1960's.

American cultural life in the year 1962 was given a boost by the interest which the first family, particularly the first lady, showed in painting, music, ballet, and literature. White House dinners, for the first time since the days of Theodore Roosevelt, were given in honor of artists and intellectuals. In addition, Mrs. Kennedy, with the help of an expert committee and many private gifts, refurnished much of the White House and made it, for the first time since it was burned by the British 150 years ago, a worthy residence for the Chief Executive. The President and his wife also enthusiastically promoted the proposed National Cultural Center in Washington, D. C., and were the prize attraction at a fund raising dinner given on November 19 to inaugurate the project. The President even added a highly qualified cultural co-ordinator, Mr. August Heckscher, to his staff.

The encouragement which the Kennedy Administration gave to the arts in the nation's capital was matched by the financial patronage which made possible the opening of the first of the new glass and concrete buildings which together will form the Lincoln Center for the

Performing Arts in New York City. Late in September, Mrs. Kennedy headed an impressive array of guests at the opening concert at Philharmonic Hall. When completed Lincoln Center will outstrip in size and importance the projected cultural center in Washington and the dozens of other such centers which are springing up all over the United States.

The desire to endow Seattle, Washington, with such a center was the main reason behind the Seattle World's Fair of 1962. About 10,000,000 people visited the Fair, the first profitable World's Fair in the United States since the one in Chicago in 1933-34. The Fair brought many people to the Pacific Northwest for the first time, and after its six months' run left the city of Seattle a whole complex of civic buildings—an opera house, a theater, a display hall and a coliseum.

The most significant event on the American literary scene in 1962 was not the ascendancy of any new writer of major importance but the disappearance of one who had graced American literature for decades. On July 6, William Faulkner died of a heart attack in his home town, Oxford, Mississippi. Faulkner had created Yoknapatawpha County and its residents to portray the South as he saw it—living on the memory of a glorious past, struggling to live by the terms of a 20th century it could not understand. A major literary figure abroad as well as in the United States, Faulkner had won the Nobel Prize for literature in 1949. The year of Faulkner's death saw another American, the novelist John Steinbeck, receive this coveted award. The award perhaps attested to the continuing vitality of American fiction, but in the year 1962 the most widely read book in the United States was *The Silent Spring,* a nonfiction work by a highly respected biologist. Miss Rachel Carson's controversial book was an attack on the poisoning of man's environment by "substances nature never invented." She presented a frightening account of the way in which chlorinated hydrocarbons such as DDT manage to find their way into the body. Since these substances are new, no one can know what they may do to humans over a long period. Apart from this danger to human life, Miss Carson foresaw a kind of chemical devastation of the soil and wild life, a "silent spring," she said, in which the only living creatures might be those strains of cockroaches, mosquitoes and flies which had adapted themselves to the ever present poison.

The popularly memorable stories of the year were those repeatedly featured in the mass circulation newspapers and magazines. In 1962 these stories were about Sonny Liston, the new world heavyweight champion; about the Kennedy clan, which received more publicity than any first family since the Roosevelts; about the romance of screen star Elizabeth Taylor and British actor Richard Burton; about the Texas multimillionaire Billie Sol Estes, who was deeply religious and who neither smoked nor drank but who swindled the farmers of Texas and the United States government out of millions of dollars; about Richard Nixon, who lost his race for the governorship of California and in his political swan song lashed out at the American press in an unseemly tirade which reminded most reporters of Harry S. Truman's political advice: "If you can't stand the heat, stay out of the kitchen"; about Ted Kennedy, the President's youngest brother, whom the voters of Massachusetts elevated to the U. S. Senate in the face of his youth, inexperience and lack of any obvious qualifications; and about Mrs. Eleanor Roosevelt, widow of America's most famous 20th-century President, whose death brought glowing tributes to a woman who personified much that was finest in the American character—its respect for fair play, its unselfishness, and its idealism and optimism.

O N November 22, 1963, John Fitzgerald Kennedy, 35th President of the United States, was struck down by an assassin's bullet in Dallas, Texas. The people of the nation and of the world were stunned by the news that this young, dynamic, and resourceful leader of the world's most powerful country had been the fated victim of a plot concocted in the demented mind of a single individual. Even as the news of this cruel turn of fate was spreading, Lyndon B. Johnson, the 36th President of the United States, was taking his oath of office. The conscience of the nation had received a staggering blow, but the continuity of its political institutions was demonstrated as the new President pledged himself to carry out the policies of the country's slain leader.

On Thursday, November 21, the President, accompanied by Mrs. Kennedy, left Washington for a two-day political tour of Texas. On the same day, in the dusk of a warm autumn afternoon, Kennedy drove through Houston's downtown streets which were lined with almost 300,000 well-wishers. He appeared buoyant and assured as he waved from his open car. On Friday morning, after enthusiastic receptions in San Antonio and Fort Worth, the President arrived in Dallas where he was scheduled to address a luncheon meeting at the Trade Mart. The eleven-mile motorcade which escorted him through the city was greeted along the way by large and cheering crowds. Kennedy, sitting in the back of an open car with his wife and Texas Governor John B. Connally and Mrs. Connally, responded warmly. At 12:30 P.M. as the motorcade approached an underpass, shots rang out. The President slumped forward, blood streaming from his head. Governor Connally, who turned at the sound of shooting, was struck by another bullet in the chest. One witness saw a rifle being withdrawn from the sixth-floor window of a nearby building. The driver of the presidental car rushed to Dallas's Parkland Hospital. There, in an emergency operating room, a team of fifteen physicians strove to save the President's life. But the effort was hopeless; he died without gaining consciousness. At 1:36 P.M. waiting reporters were told that "President John F. Kennedy died at approximately 1 o'clock Central Standard Time . . . of a gunshot wound in the brain."

Scarcely more than an hour later, Lyndon B. Johnson, flanked by Mrs. Kennedy and Mrs. Johnson, took the oath of office aboard the presidential jet. Immediately after the oath was taken, the plane, also carrying the body of the late President, took off for Washington.

The routine life of the nation came to a halt. As word of the assassination was flashed across the country,

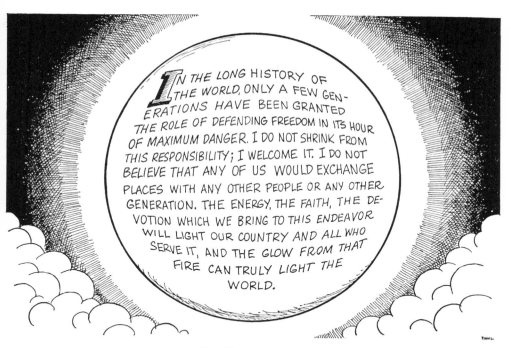

IN THE LONG HISTORY OF THE WORLD, ONLY A FEW GENERATIONS HAVE BEEN GRANTED THE ROLE OF DEFENDING FREEDOM IN ITS HOUR OF MAXIMUM DANGER. I DO NOT SHRINK FROM THIS RESPONSIBILITY; I WELCOME IT. I DO NOT BELIEVE THAT ANY OF US WOULD EXCHANGE PLACES WITH ANY OTHER PEOPLE OR ANY OTHER GENERATION. THE ENERGY, THE FAITH, THE DEVOTION WHICH WE BRING TO THIS ENDEAVOR WILL LIGHT OUR COUNTRY AND ALL WHO SERVE IT, AND THE GLOW FROM THAT FIRE CAN TRULY LIGHT THE WORLD.

"Profile in Courage"
Dahl in *The Boston Herald*

"Another Helmsman"
Little in *The Nashville Tennessean*

there was first disbelief, then consternation, and finally grief. Millions of Americans grouped around radios and television sets as every major station in the nation abandoned its customary programs to a coverage of the macabre events in Dallas and the mournful events in Washington.

The search for the assassin was brief. Dallas police quickly arrested Lee Harvey Oswald, a 24-year-old former Marine. The evidence that Oswald was the sniper who had murdered the President was massive, but he steadfastly denied it throughout long hours of interrogation undergone without the aid of counsel. Oswald's motives, however, were unfathomable. That he was emotionally unstable became clearer with every new piece of evidence unearthed about him. His family was poor and rootless (his father died before Lee was born); he was diagnosed as a problem child during a brief period spent in New York City as a youth; he was attracted to Marxism in his teens; he left school at 17 to join the Marines; he was released from active duty in 1959 and soon thereafter showed up in Moscow where he announced his intention of becoming a Soviet citizen. The Russians were as reluctant to accept him as the United States was willing to lose him, and Oswald, disillusioned by long hours of work in a Russian factory at low pay, returned to the United States, accompanied by a Russian wife. So far as anyone knew, Oswald bore no animus toward President Kennedy. His motives doubtless lay in the dark and twisted recesses of an insane mind, but no one will ever know for sure. As he was being moved from the Dallas city jail to the county prison, some 48 hours after he was arrested, a man stepped out of a crowd of newsmen, shoved a revolver into Oswald's side and fired one shot. Oswald groaned and slumped to the floor unconscious. The Dallas police had permitted TV coverage of Oswald's transfer and the shooting occurred before millions of startled viewers. He was rushed to Parkland Hospital, to which President Kennedy had been taken two days earlier, where he died without regaining consciousness. His assailant was Jack Ruby, a 52-year-old Dallas night-club operator.

On Saturday, November 23, the late President's body lay in state in the East Room of the White House. Members of his family and government dignitaries filed by the closed, flag-draped coffin. On Sunday, Kennedy's body was borne on a caisson drawn by six white horses from the White House to the Capitol. The route of the cortege was lined by thousands of grief-benumbed citizens and millions more watched the procession on television. All day and throughout the night some 250,000 people filed in silence past the bier in the Capitol rotunda.

The next day the body was taken back to the White House and from there to St. Matthew's Cathedral. Leaders from all over the world, in Washington to pay tribute to the dead President, joined the Kennedy family and American dignitaries in the walk behind the flag-decked coffin to the Cathedral. After a Requiem Mass at St. Matthew's, the cortege made its way to Arlington National Cemetery. There, as the doleful sound of taps echoed through the sun-lit Virginia hills, the President's body was lowered to its final resting place.

The eulogies which were delivered on the days after Kennedy's death eloquently expressed the esteem in which his countrymen held him. But only time can determine his place in history. Shock at the brutal nature of his death; grief that such an able leader should die so young; horror at the hate that still lurks in the country; indignation that the leader of the world's showcase of democracy should be struck down by an assassin's bullets; uncertainty about the future of the policies which he so steadfastly supported; anxiety about the impact of his death on the country's future—all these things preclude balanced judgment.

Kennedy was President, after all, for less than three years. What he could accomplish was thus limited and history will judge him, as it has judged Lincoln, not only for what he did but also for what he might have done. Some historians argue that Lincoln's greatness consisted in large measure in his magnanimous policy toward the defeated South; had he lived, they say, the agonies of Reconstruction might have been avoided. Greatness may be attributed to Kennedy, similarly, not so much for what he did as for what he might have done. Kennedy had a keen insight into America's problems and offered statesmanlike solutions to them. Speaking in Chicago in March, 1963, for example, he proposed to use the affluence that technology has produced to repair the human ravages it has created. But he added pointedly that whether or not this could be done depended on the will of Congress and of the people. Had he lived and been elected to a second term he might conceivably have exercised the moral leadership necessary to bend the public will toward the accomplishment of his goals.

Such speculative judgments, on the other hand, may be summarily dismissed by future historians who may choose to assess Kennedy on the basis of what he did rather than on what he might have done. He thus may be ranked as a great President because he combined superb gifts as a politician with the elevating humanity and sound judgment which are usually regarded as the hallmarks of statesmanship. They may point, moreover, to his impressive accomplishments—to the firmness and skill with which he handled the explosive civil rights question, the sureness and deftness with which he forced the Russians to remove the missiles from Cuba without bringing on a nuclear war, or to the conclusion of a test ban treaty which, whether or not it lasts, was a great accomplishment of civilized statecraft. These accomplishments alone, it may be argued, are sufficient to assure Kennedy a secure niche in the presidential hall of fame.

Whatever they may say in praise of Kennedy, it is certain that historians will also probe his shortcomings. The criticisms which were made of him during his presidency offer a clue to what may be said of him years after his death. His bitterest critics were conservatives of the "radical right" and die-hard segregationists of the South. But he was also criticized by liberals who charged that he tired too quickly of beckoning people to new horizons and too soon became defensively conservative. Liberal Democrats, moreover, accused him of doing nothing to assist them against the conservatives in the Senate. Some practical politicians, paradoxically enough, said that the President was too far-sighted, his mind too penetrating. He saw the things that were basically wrong and the things that needed to be done, such critics argued, but, taking as he did the long view, he failed sufficiently to emphasize the day-to-day problems or to rouse the people.

Lyndon B. Johnson at once pledged himself to carry out the policies of his predecessor. However successfully he might do so, it was certain (as newspaper writers repeated time and again) that the Johnson "style" would be markedly different. Kennedy personified the new and novel in national life; Johnson, the traditional. Kennedy represented the urban, industrial, and international-minded Northeast; Johnson, the rural, agricultural, and regional interests of the Southwest. Kennedy surrounded himself with college professors and felt most at home in the company of intellectuals; Johnson's closest associates have been professional politicians. Kennedy had a wide knowledge of history and literature; Johnson reads few books and is not a conventionally cultured man.

No President of this century has assumed office with

more extensive political experience than Johnson. For a quarter of a century his life has been spent in the thick of Washington politics, first as secretary of a Texas Congressman, then as Congressman in his own right, next as Senator, and, finally, as Vice President. At the time of his election to the House in 1937 he was regarded as a fiery New Dealer; by the time he was elected to the Senate in 1948 he was regarded as a conservative. Whatever his political philosophy, his ability was unmistakable. Within four years of entering the Senate he was elected his party's floor leader, and as Senate majority leader during the last six years of the Eisenhower Administration he ran the Senate with a strong hand (by far too strong for some of his colleagues). Johnson's parliamentary skill was such that it entitles him to rank with Henry Clay and Daniel Webster, Robert Taft and Arthur Vandenberg as one of the immortals of the U. S. Senate.

Johnson went to the 1960 Democratic National Convention with 300 delegates pledged to him. That his candidacy failed to inspire more enthusiasm may be attributed to the popular belief that he was more a professional politician than a potential statesman. Traditionally, Americans have favored the gifted amateur over the professional politician as President. At any event, it was soon evident at the Convention that the Kennedy bandwagon could not be stopped by Johnson or any other contender. Johnson settled for second place on the ticket and presumably resigned himself to a position of declining importance in national politics. On November 22, 1963, he became the first great congressional leader of either house (James K. Polk perhaps excepted) to become President.

Five days after he took the oath of office Johnson appeared before a joint session of Congress. In a brief but forceful speech he spoke with sorrow and admiration of President Kennedy and pledged himself to continue the Kennedy program, domestic and foreign. Civil rights and tax legislation, Johnson said, should be speedily enacted "to honor the President's memory and to continue his program." The late President's foreign program was endorsed point by point, and Johnson promised to honor America's commitments "from South Vietnam to West Berlin," to develop United States military power, to seek areas of agreement, even with adversaries, to expand trade, to be faithful to the principles and the organization of the United Nations, and to help other nations, especially those in Latin America.

During the few weeks he was President in the year 1963, Johnson was not forced to make foreign policy decisions of any consequence. During this respite (which was sure to be brief), Johnson turned his attention to the area in which he was most experienced—Capitol Hill. Most of Kennedy's legislative program was still locked up in Congress and Johnson set himself the seemingly herculean task of prying it out.

Some thirteen months earlier President Kennedy, in his State of the Union Message, had given Congress a reassuring review of the world situation and had argued that American leadership of the free world must be based on economic advances at home. In the weeks that followed, he sent Congress a number of special messages which proposed legislation dealing with the aged and with youth, with mental illness and with health, with education and agriculture, and with taxes and economic growth.

In his message on "aiding our senior citizens," the President renewed his familiar demand for a "medicare" program for people of 65 and over, and proposed such other measures as better housing and retraining to aid the country's 17,000,000 old people. In his message on the country's youth, he reaffirmed his confidence in the work of the Peace Corps and recommended the establishment of its domestic equivalent, a National Service Corps, to deal with the problem of unemployment among the young.

In the first of a series of messages on health, the President asked for a bold, new approach to mental illness, the first such request ever sent to Congress. To reduce the 800,000 or more patients who overcrowd mental institutions, he recommended the creation of community mental health centers; to reduce the proportion of the population suffering from mental retardation, he asked that more money be spent on maternity and child welfare services for poor families. In a second message on health, he called on the Federal government to provide financial help for medical and nursing students and to assist in modernizing and improving hospitals and nursing homes.

To deal with the problems of American education, which is falling lamentably below its potential, Kennedy proposed a four-year program of Federal aid to those states which could show that they really needed help. To handle the perennial agricultural problem, he outlined means of reducing the amount of money which the government spends on price supports, recommended measures for providing more food for needy people at home and abroad, and offered a program for improving living conditions in rural areas.

The most important of the President's proposals, and the one to which he gave top priority, was a tax cut. Kennedy recommended a reduction of $13.5 billion in taxes, to be spread over three years. Such a reduction, he said, would help to provide Americans with 2,000,000 new jobs each year, would make the economy grow faster, and would thus be the surest and soundest way to achieve a balanced budget. In view of the record budget of $98.8 billion which was requested for fiscal 1964 and the anticipated deficit of $11.9 billion, his argument confused many of those people unskilled in the intricacies of economics. A plan which would cut personal income taxes and reduce taxes on business and yet balance rather than further unbalance the budget appeared to them as little short of miraculous.

To the President and his economic advisers the arguments in favor of a tax cut were persuasive. The chief domestic problem in the United States, as they saw the situation at the beginning of the year, was a sluggish economy. This could possibly mean, they believed, a growing dependence on defense contracts or on hand-outs from the Federal government for an increasing number of Americans. To the Kennedy Administration the solution to the problem of a stagnant economy was a tax cut. The idea behind it was to put more cash in the hands of individuals, who presumably would spend it on consumer goods, and in the hands of corporations, which could be expected to use the money for new plants and equipment. This would mean, the Administration contended, more jobs and greater business activity and, in the end, higher total tax collections.

Possibly no one expected Congress to proceed briskly on a subject as complicated as tax reform or on programs as controversial as most of those the President suggested. But it was widely predicted in January that the congressional session would end by mid-summer after presenting the President with some of the major acts he had requested, the tax cut among them. Congressmen, however, were obviously in no hurry. When they adjourned for a ten-day Easter recess, for example, their record of accomplishment on major bills was practically nil, and from then on they talked no longer of a summer adjournment. (One student of congressional history remarked that the unusual length of congressional sessions in recent years should be attributed to air conditioning).

Despite the snail-like pace at which Congress proceeded, it appeared likely in early summer that at least a bill reducing taxes would be passed before adjournment. The President's success in winning the support of Southern Democrats for his economic program appeared to have insured its implementation. This well-laid plan was shattered, however, when on June 19, Kennedy submitted to Congress proposals for the strongest civil rights bill in American history and assigned it a top priority. The Southerners now undertook a campaign of obstruction and delay that put not only the tax cut but all of his program in jeopardy. Could Kennedy have controlled events, he doubtless would have deferred civil rights legislation until 1964, but events soon were propelling him. By June civil rights had become the nation's number one problem and had almost totally eclipsed every other domestic issue.

The racial outbursts in the summer of 1963 were the most serious in the country's history. They came 100 years after the Emancipation Proclamation and emphasized how little has been done over the past century to assure American Negroes the economic and political equality without which genuine freedom is impossible. They revealed, moreover, that the rank and file of American Negroes have thrown off the subservient mentality of slavery and are no longer willing to be second-class citizens. This new-found militancy led many observers to describe 1963 as the year of the "Negro Revolution."

Negro discontent was not confined to the South but

was nation-wide. While the focus of the movement in the South was on voting rights, school integration, and an end to discrimination in stores, restaurants, hotels, and other businesses serving the public, the focus in the North was on economic opportunity. The 20,000,000 American Negroes are the underdeveloped one-tenth of the nation. For the individual Negro, North as well as South, the dearth of economic opportunity is perhaps that aspect of oppression which causes the greatest personal suffering.

The Negro protest began in Birmingham, Ala., a city which has a history of brutality and violence in race relations and which has been described by Dr. Martin Luther King, the Negro leader, as "the most segregated large city in the United States." The demonstrations which began there on April 3 appeared at first to be following a pattern that had become familiar in the South over the past few years—protest marches by a few hundred Negro adults, warnings by the police against unauthorized parades, and a number of arrests. But on May 2, the demonstrations took a more serious turn.

Young Negro demonstrators (mostly youths in their teens, some even younger) marched in groups of about fifty toward City Hall, singing the integration hymn "We Shall Overcome." Although the police threw up barricades and made arrests by the hundreds, the demonstrators were not belligerent. When stopped by the police, some of them fell to their knees and prayed; when arrested, they ran cheerfully to the buses that were used to transport them to jail. But on the following day, the mood grew uglier. The Birmingham police used fire hoses and police dogs to break up the parades, and the demonstrators retaliated by throwing stones and bottles at police from the roofs of buildings. The timing of the demonstrations, as Attorney General Robert Kennedy said, may have been open to question (a more moderate city government had been elected although its installation was being held up by a legal wrangle), and the decision to expose young children to the risks of street demonstrations may have been deplorable. But whatever mistakes in tactics the Negroes made, no humane citizen could fail to be shocked at photographs of a police dog, teeth bared, attacking an unnamed Negro boy or of a policeman kneeling on a Negro woman's throat. The conscience of the nation was aroused; the image of America abroad was badly tarnished.

The President walked warily, however. On the one hand, he wished to avoid a clash between Federal and state authorities which might turn Southerners against the Democratic party; on the other, he wanted to convince Negro voters in both the North and the South that he was doing all he could to advance their cause. On May 10, partly because of his backing and encouragement, a truce was arranged between Negro leaders and Birmingham's civic and business leaders. The latter agreed to the creation of a biracial committee to keep open a channel of communication, promised that within three months the color bar would disappear from lunch

counters, lavatories, and drinking fountains, and agreed
that within two months a start would be made to open
some nonmenial jobs in the big shops to Negroes. The
agreement, though it may have given the Negroes all
they could expect, was not extravagantly generous. Nor
did it put an end to demonstrations and violence. Only
a day or so later, renewed violence led the President to
prepare for Federal intervention by ordering 3,000
soldiers to posts near Birmingham, ready for action if
necessary.

Heartened by the limited desegregation which Negroes
in Birmingham had won and shocked into action by
the strong-arm tactics of the Birmingham police, tens
of thousands of Negroes across the country turned out
in protest demonstrations and rallies. In mid-May, just
as the tension in Birmingham was relaxing, there were
clashes between Negroes and whites in Nashville, Tenn.,
unsuccessful demonstrations in Jackson, Miss., and successful protests in Raleigh and Greensboro, N. C. During the last week of May the racial battle intensified. In
Jackson, Miss., a Negro was kicked in the face for sitting
at a segregated lunch counter; in Tallahassee, Fla., hundreds of Negro students were arrested for demonstrating
against all-white theaters; and in Philadelphia, police
scuffled with Negroes who were protesting job discrimination.

The summer of 1963 was aptly termed the summer of
Negro discontent. On July 25, for example, the *New
York Times* carried 28 stories dealing with various

aspects of the movement. One-half of the items were about pickets, demonstrations, and arrests. At Cambridge, on Maryland's eastern shore, the withdrawal of National Guardsmen who had been sent to end racial disturbances was followed by a night of wild rioting, with roving bands shooting from cars. In Savannah, Ga., the police used tear gas to break up a Negro mob which then fanned out through the city throwing bottles and stones. In Charleston, S. C., police were showered with debris when they tried to disperse a Negro mob.

In the meantime, as has been seen, the President had responded to the growing demand for stringent civil rights legislation. On June 19, he sent to Congress a civil rights program which was designed to atone, in part, for a century of neglect. It called for: (1) A guarantee of equal access to all public facilities related to interstate commerce—hotels, restaurants, stores, filling stations, and the like. (2) Authority for the Attorney General to initiate legal suits on behalf of individuals who complained of civil rights violations, principally in school desegregation cases. (3) A broad attack on racial unemployment problems by outlawing job discrimination in federally supported projects and providing Federal funds for vocational training. The most controversial of the proposals was the first, the so-called public accommodations section. The Administration found the constitutional basis for banning discrimination against Negro customers in the Federal government's authority to regulate interstate commerce. Many Republicans objected to this approach on the grounds that the Democrats over the past two decades have used such a broad interpretation of the commerce clause to encroach on private business and the rights of the states. They would have preferred to base the proposed measure on that section of the 14th Amendment to the Constitution which guarantees equal protection of the laws to all citizens.

From the outcry which the President's proposals immediately provoked, it was apparent that the legislative road to a civil rights act would be long and rough. Southern Congressmen, for example, called it "beyond the realm of reason," a "grasp for power," an invitation for "mob action and public disorder." Hearings on the bill were held for several weeks and, although there was no marked progress, it was generally agreed that a civil rights bill would be passed before Congress adjourned. Slowly, however, the mood of Congress and the country began to change. The Negro demonstrations were antagonizing many Northern whites who previously had been either lukewarm or apathetic to the Negro cause. Congressmen's mail bags were soon filled with letters denouncing the President's proposals; nation-wide public-opinion polls revealed that a majority of the whites believed the Negroes were pushing too hard and too fast in seeking equal rights.

It was to impress on Congress the moderateness, intensity, and seriousness of their purpose that American Negroes staged the largest and most impressive demonstration in U.S. history. The idea of a march on Washington was conceived in June when President Kennedy submitted his civil rights proposals to Congress. The march was scheduled for late August in the expectation that it would coincide with the attempt of Southern Senators to talk the bill to death. Although it was soon apparent that no legislation could be expected until autumn, if then, it was hoped that the demonstration would at least hasten congressional action. The purpose of the march, furthermore, was broadened, and its official title became the "March on Washington for Jobs and Freedom."

On August 28, more than 200,000 people, most of them Negroes, converged on Washington. The precautions which the Commissioners of the District of Columbia had taken to guard against violence appeared absurd, for the marchers, conscious that the eyes of the world were upon them, behaved with dignity and decorum. The march from the Washington Monument to the Lincoln Memorial, along tree-lined Constitution Avenue, was a quiet and solemn, yet joyful, procession. Throughout a long afternoon of speeches delivered at the Lincoln Memorial, the crowd was occasionally enthusiastic, sometimes bored, and consistently patient. By late afternoon, the leaders of the march were congratulating themselves over the almost unbelievable absence of incidents.

Yet the march was no unqualified success. It is doubtful that it had any important impact on the battle in Congress over civil rights, and it would be difficult to prove that it helped to cure the national disease of racial bias. But it was a compelling demonstration of the determination of American Negroes to secure the equal rights so long denied them. It was a phase of their continuing struggle, rather than the climax.

That this struggle would be long, arduous, and perhaps bloody was demonstrated by the renewed outbreak of violence in Birmingham. On September 15, dynamiters blew up a Negro church during Sunday School and killed four Negro girls. As the news spread, there were riots and other violence. Police killed a Negro boy, 16, who had been hurling stones at white youths in cars flying Confederate flags, and a 13-year-old Negro boy was slain by two white youths. In Negro neighborhoods gunfire was heard and fires flared. Mayor Albert Boutwell broadcast appeals for an end to "this senseless reign of terror" and Governor Wallace called the dynamiters "madmen." But Southerners as well as Northerners suggested that the Governor examine his own conscience. His attempt to close the public schools to both whites and Negroes rather than obey a court order demanding the registration of a few Negro students, they said, had set an example of lawlessness that may have sparked the murder.

Birmingham clearly revealed what the events in other places also demonstrated. Apostles of nonviolence and moderate Negro organizations, including the National Association for the Advancement of Colored People, were in danger of being swept aside by growing Negro impatience for results. Many Negroes obviously were fed up with the gradual approach, disillusioned by counsels of moderation, and angry at unfilled promises. It seemed to many people that time was running out. Only by a great awakening of the conscience of the country and the exercise of moral leadership by its officials would tragedy be averted and the race problem solved.

Neither Negro protests nor the proddings of the President, however, were enough to inspire Congress with any sense of urgency. As the fall wore on, the civil rights bill was still in the hands of the House Judiciary Committee. There was conflict over it between Republicans and Democrats, between Democrats and Democrats, and between Republicans and Republicans. The problem was to devise a bill which both the Northern Democrats and the bulk of the Republicans would support, for without Republican support it would be impossible to crush the inevitable Southern resistance in the Senate. Finally, late in October, the House Judiciary Committee approved a bill that not only met Administration specifications but also satisfied both liberal Democrats and the Republicans. This political feat involved no compromise on civil rights and, indeed, in one respect the measure which emerged was a stronger one than the Administration originally had proposed. It provided for a Fair Employment Practices Commission to enforce a ban on racial discrimination in employment, a controversial proposal which the Administration wanted to leave to a separate bill. But passage by the Judiciary Committee was, after all, only the first and least formidable of the legislative hurdles which a Civil Rights Act had to surmount. At the time of Kennedy's death on November 22, the bill was bogged down in the Rules Committee, which controls the flow of legislative traffic to the floor of the House of Representatives, and if the committee's powerful chairman, Howard W. Smith of Virginia, could have his way it would never emerge.

President Kennedy's economic program fared no better in Congress than his civil rights proposals. After nine months of labor, the House produced a tax cut bill which was acceptable to leaders of both parties in the House but which was not altogether pleasing to anyone. Economists who wished taxes to be reduced as early as possible in order to stimulate the economy were unhappy that the committee's bill provided no tax relief until 1964; union leaders said that the amount of relief provided for low-income families was inadequate; businessmen argued that the rate on corporate income was not reduced enough; advocates of comprehensive tax reform complained that most of the reforms recommended in the President's original program had been considerably diluted or jettisoned altogether. Nevertheless, the tax bill, calling for an $11 billion tax cut in personal and corporate income taxes during 1964 and 1965, was passed by the House in September by a vote of 271 to 155. It faced an uncertain future in the Senate, however, where Senator Harry F. Byrd, Democrat of Virginia and chairman of the Finance Committee, was neither convinced nor even impressed by the President's argument that a tax cut would give vigor to the economy and prevent future economic downturns.

Many Americans were inclined to agree with Senator Byrd. When the Administration proposed its economic program in January, the economy was sluggish and the tax program was justified on the grounds that it would speed up recovery. By the time it was approved by the House and went to the Senate, however, the economy was booming.

The year's economic statistics told a tale of prosperity and abundance. Business activity in the first quarter of the year, for example, exceeded even the most optimistic forecasts—consumer spending was high, business outlays were heavy, inventories were being built up, and government spending continued to mount. Signs of an economic upturn were even more encouraging in the summer, usually a period of doldrums for business and industry. The gross national product—broadest of all economic indicators—soared, industrial production increased, with key industries such as automobiles and steel turning in performances ranging from sensational to encouraging, personal income went up, factory orders rose, and retail sales improved.

The economic story of 1963 as a whole might be told by the headlines in the "National Economic Review," published by the *New York Times* early in 1964. Sample headlines read as follows: "Nation Poised for New Surge of Prosperity"; "Railroads See the Gains of '63 as

Only a Beginning"; "Airlines Chalk up Revenue Increase"; "Rubber Industry Passes $10 Billion"; "Chemicals Reach Record Again"; "Steel Achieves a Breakthrough"; "Further Construction Expansion Expected." To round out this economic success story, President Johnson announced at the end of the year that the nation had reached a pinnacle of prosperity unmatched in the history of the Union—the value of the nation's goods and services had soared to the spectacular rate of $600 billion a year.

How, in the midst of such prosperity, could economists fret about the performance of the economy? Why, even as the boom accelerated, had President Kennedy continued to press Congress for a tax cut in order to spur economic growth? The answer is to be found in a set of statistics, ignored in the preceding picture of the American economic glow, dealing with the nation's major economic problem, unemployment. Even as President Johnson was summoning Americans to look up at the peaks of prosperity, the Department of Labor was pointing out that the rate of unemployment was higher in December than at the beginning of the year, that 30,000,000 Americans were living in poverty, and that one out of every five young Negroes was out of work. The average jobless rate for the year 1963 was 5.7 percent; in more human terms this meant over 4,000,000 unemployed. It was this unemployment in the midst of prosperity, this poverty in the midst of plenty, that disturbed thoughtful Americans, among them President Kennedy.

Speaking in Chicago in March, Kennedy said that unemployment was the major concern of the United States in the prosperous 1960's as it had been in the depressed 1930's. His comparison between the two decades was instructive. Some twenty years ago Franklin D. Roosevelt's forecast of 60,000,000 jobs was ridiculed; yet by June, 1963, some 70,000,000 people were at work. On the other hand, full employment appeared as difficult to achieve in the 1960's as it had seemed impossible thirty years earlier; in June, 1963, some 6 percent of the labor force was out of work and there were 39 major industrial areas with "substantial unemployment." What was responsible for the plight of American labor? In his Chicago speech, the President blamed it on the fast advance of technology in farming and industry, combined with the tidal wave of war babies flooding the labor market. Whatever the cause, the cure would appear to be the simple one of training the grown-up war babies and providing them with jobs. The paradox is, however, that advancing technology has made their labor superfluous.

"The world today is not the world of Adam Smith," Walter Reuther, head of the Automobile Workers Union, has remarked. "It is the world of the computer and the automated plant." Automation, the replacement of men by machines, is the specter that haunts labor leaders and government officials alike. Only a small part of the country's productive equipment has thus far been automated. But automatic machines can, and perhaps soon will on a large scale, make and roll steel, mine coal, weave cloth, sort and grade fruit, sort bank checks and notes, keep records, direct traffic, translate languages, assemble typewriters, drive passenger trains by tape, and make machine tools by numbers. The progress of automation was sure to accelerate during the 1960's, the very decade when some 26,000,000 new workers (almost half again as many as graduated from the country's schools in the 1950's) are expected to enter the labor market. It is estimated, moreover, that almost one-third (or 7,500,000) of them will be those who have dropped out of high school and whom almost no one will want to employ.

These gloomy figures depressed no one more than they did the leaders of organized labor. In November, George Meany, president of the American Federation of Labor and Congress of Industrial Organizations, told his organization's biennial convention in New York that the capitalist system might destroy itself unless something drastic was done to prevent automation ("this curse," as he called it) from throwing millions of workers on the scrap heap.

The giant strides made by American labor unions during recent decades appeared, superficially at least, to belie such a dismal prediction. Twenty-five years ago labor chiefs were still fighting for recognition, carrying out sit-down strikes, and fighting battles with industry's private armies. Today they have long-term contracts with the largest industries in the country, have won for their members high wages (the average factory wage is over $100 a week), and have provided them with security against illness and old age. Union delegates, moreover, now assemble in the plush hotels of Puerto Rico or Miami for their annual conventions, and union leaders sit in glass and marble headquarters which are as impressive as the headquarters of billion dollar corporations.

Despite these trappings of success, labor leaders have good reasons for being deeply concerned about the future of unionism in the United States. The revelation of corruption in some unions and the hostility of some conservatives are not the chief sources of their concern. It is rather the effects which automation has on union membership. The tens of thousands of workers who are losing their jobs are being replaced by a few technicians who have little interest in joining unions. As the technicians replace blue-collar workers, management has less and less to fear from strikes.

The difficulties of labor unions in trying to protect their members against the tolls of automation were demonstrated in the year's record of collective bargaining. Technological change was a large factor in a five-week longshoremen's strike, which immobilized American shipping at an estimated loss of $25 million a day, and which was settled early in the year only after a board appointed by the President laid down the terms. It was also a major element in prolonged newspaper strikes in New York City and Cleveland, as it was in labor conflicts on the airlines. But the most dramatic instance of the problems that technological change can create for organized labor was the railroad labor dispute.

At issue in the dispute, which already had dragged on for four wearying years, was the demand of the railroad companies that they be allowed to eliminate the "featherbedding" which forces them to employ many unnecessary workmen—firemen on modern engines where there are no fires to stoke, for example. This, they claimed, would save the railroads as much as $600 million a year. The unions, on the other hand, staunchly resisted such a demand, for the obvious reason that it would mean the loss of some 65,000 jobs.

Three times during 1963 the announcement of the railroads that they were going to dispense with archaic work rules was answered by a union call for a nationwide strike which would have tied up 95 percent of the country's rail traffic. Three times a national economic crisis was averted at the last minute by the Federal government. Finally, on August 28, just eight hours before a strike deadline, Congress, for the first time in a peacetime dispute, imposed arbitration. Few Congressmen wished to set a precedent so dangerous to the future of free collective bargaining but every other alternative obviously had been exhausted.

The act barred a strike for 180 days and called for a seven-man board made up of two representatives each

of management and labor and three of the public to
settle the two central questions, removal of firemen and
train crew reductions. Within 90 days the board was to
rule on the companies' proposals that those firemen who
are no longer needed on diesel engines be dismissed and
that the number of similarly superfluous men on train
crews be cut back drastically. The board's decisions were
to remain in force for two years. The other issues in the
dispute were left to further private bargaining and a
strike over them was prohibited until a month after the
board's ruling on the major matters should take effect.

Congressmen were the more chagrined at playing the
uncongenial role of strike-breakers because they knew
that they had solved only temporarily the four-year-old
railway labor problem. They also knew that they had
not solved at all the two issues in the railway dispute
which are the most important problems in labor-man-
agement relations in the United States. These are what
to do about "national emergency strikes" and what to
do about the problems presented by automation. As the
law now stands, a strike which creates a national emergency can be postponed for a time but it cannot be prevented. As to automation, most Americans agree that
it should not be allowed to create severe economic
hardship for individuals, but this requires vastly more
thought and action than have yet been taken.

At the beginning of the year 1963, President Kennedy and his advisers were cautiously optimistic about
the year's prospects in foreign relations. From Havana

to Hanoi, the United States was seeking to win friends and to influence people. In Latin America, the Administration was busily throwing out broad hints that even an extreme left-wing regime in Cuba would be acceptable to it, provided that it was not just a Soviet puppet; in Africa, the United States was enjoying the approval of many leaders because of its firm support of the United Nations force in the Congo; in Asia, America was winning friends by helping India against China; in Europe, President Kennedy's vision of a grand alliance uniting the nations of the Atlantic community was making progress; and in Russian-United States relations, the President was retaining the initiative which he had seized from Khrushchev in October, 1962.

The major problems dividing East and West—the unification of Germany, the arms race, war in Southeast Asia, strife in the Middle East, conflict in Africa—remained as persistent and intractable in the year 1963 as in previous years. But there was a "pause" (to use a favorite journalistic expression of the year) in the Cold War. It was perhaps this breathing spell which permitted the boiling up of conflicts between Russia and the United States and their respective allies. General de Gaulle, for example, presented a much more serious threat to Allied unity than ever before, and the Sino-Soviet quarrel reached a new intensity. To some foreign policy experts it appeared that the United States and Russia were drifting into an uneasy *détente* because of these difficulties; to other commentators, it seemed that Russia was only playing the United States for a sucker and they accordingly urged that the country prop up its rapidly deteriorating Western Alliance.

The Alliance had begun to crumble before the year was even two weeks old. On January 14, General de Gaulle proclaimed his unalterable opposition to a United States proposal for the formation of a multilateral nuclear force within the North Atlantic Treaty Organization. Although fourteen other members of NATO were generally disposed favorably toward the project, French cooperation was essential to its success. Scarcely two weeks later, France vetoed Britain's application for membership in the Common Market, ending sixteen months of painful negotiations. The other members of the Common Market—West Germany, Italy, Belgium, the Netherlands, and Luxemburg—bowed to General de Gaulle's will rather than break up their association. By these moves De Gaulle blocked the development of a common policy for NATO, upset President Kennedy's "grand design," threw the British economic program into confusion and destroyed Allied unity. During the months which followed, the Allies scarcely attempted to conceal the ill feeling among them. The French spoke disparagingly of the "Anglo-Saxons," and President Kennedy made barbed comments about good faith among allies.

The rift in the Western Alliance doubtless was owing to many factors—to the decline of the United States as the world's only superpower, to the nuclear stalemate between East and West, to Britain's declining strength, and to the economic resurgence of Continental Europe. But the fact that in every quarrel of consequence within the Alliance De Gaulle was one of the partners suggests that the French President was primarily responsible for the disruption.

Three major issues, as has been suggested, divided the Western Alliance—a political argument, a military dispute, and an economic disagreement.

The political argument took the form of a French revolt against American leadership of the alliance. It was based on De Gaulle's differences with the United States on certain key issues, notably on the wisdom of negotiations with the Soviet Union and on the role that France and other members of the North Atlantic Alliance should play in the defense of Europe. There was also a fundamental collision between his concept of "independent" European powers loosely grouped under French leadership and the American concept of a politically integrated Europe, including Britain, bound together in close alliance with the United States. To De Gaulle, Europe could in time develop an identity of its own only if other European nations followed the lead of France in asserting their military and political independence. He thus emphasized France's right to take an individual course in finding solutions to such pressing international problems as the war in Vietnam or East-West relations.

The military issue involved the general question of

Western defense, and the particular questions arising out of President de Gaulle's insistence that France develop an independent nuclear deterrent and also, as we have seen, his opposition to the U. S. proposal for a multilateral nuclear force. To De Gaulle, the benefits of an independent nuclear force were twofold: It would guarantee France a measure of protection against Soviet military blackmail if the United States should lose interest in protecting Europe, and it would enhance French power and influence in Europe. From the American viewpoint, French policy only intensified the desire of other members of the alliance to become nuclear powers and greatly enhanced the danger of nuclear war. The poison of nuclear ambition, the United States insisted, ultimately would undermine the European unity so laboriously achieved.

To counter De Gaulle's plan the United States offered to share, to a limited extent, its nuclear monopoly. The Administration suggested a force of surface ships with American missiles and international crews under NATO command. American officials believed that such a multilateral force ("MLF," it was called) could provide a strong military basis for political unification of the Atlantic community. European response to "MLF" was mixed—General de Gaulle's scorn for the project was described as epic, West Germany was enthusiastic, and Britain was hesitant.

The chief economic issue dividing the Western Alliance stemmed from De Gaulle's concept of an exclusive

Continental grouping independent of Britain and the United States. Partly as a result of the De Gaulle approach, the Common Market adopted restrictionist policies toward the outside world that threatened serious economic conflicts with the United States and Britain.

President Kennedy continued to believe in the ideal of Atlantic interdependence which he had expressed in his speech in Philadelphia on July 4, 1962, and continued to hope for a cohesive and united Europe as this country's Atlantic partner. But Americans found that it was easier to deal with a Europe which was economically sick, as it was in the late 1940's and the 1950's, than with a Europe which, thanks in part to American help, was in glowing health. Many Americans, furthermore, were disillusioned by the failure of European nations to carry their share of the financial burdens of the Western Alliance. It appeared to them unfair for Europeans to assume that the United States would continue indefinitely to put 11 percent of its gross national product into defense and foreign aid while some of Europe's most prosperous nations were doing proportionately only half as much. Such disparity of effort was, according to this viewpoint, the more disturbing in light of the fact that in some parts of Western Europe there is now less poverty and unemployment than in many parts of the United States. Was it not time, it was asked, for the United States to allocate more of its resources to the solution of domestic problems such as unemployment, housing, transportation, and race?

To offset General de Gaulle's bid for European leadership President Kennedy decided late in June to make a ten-day tour of Western Europe. His purpose was both to reaffirm the American commitment to Europe's freedom and to encourage its leaders to cooperate with the United States in rescuing Atlantic unity from the rising tides of European nationalism that were threatening to engulf it.

The highlight of the President's trip was his tour of West Germany. His talks with German officials were not without friction, but they indicated, much to Kennedy's satisfaction, that Chancellor Adenauer's heir, Ludwig Erhard, would not only contribute realistically to a reduction of East-West tensions but would be far less receptive than his predecessor to De Gaulle's program for Franco-German hegemony of an independent Europe. The President's trip, moreover, was a personal triumph. The streets of Cologne and Bonn, and the highway leading in from the cities' common airport, were lined with more than a million cheering Germans; in West Berlin —100 miles inside Communist territory—his welcome was even more tumultuous. Kennedy, it was widely believed, had dispelled the doubts raised by General de Gaulle about the reliability of the U. S. pledge to defend Western Europe (and Germany, in particular) against Soviet aggression.

The President visited other countries before returning

to Washington on July 3. But Ireland was a sentimental excursion; he was in Britain for only 24 hours, long enough to talk only briefly with Prime Minister Harold Macmillan; and in Italy he had to be circumspect because of an Italian political crisis. The climax of his Italian tour was his private audience with Pope Paul VI, who on June 21 had been named the 262nd supreme pontiff of the Roman Catholic Church in succession to Pope John XXIII.

Before leaving Naples for home, Kennedy made a speech in which he emphasized Western strength and unity and assured his audience that "no ally will abandon the interests of another to achieve a spurious *détente*." The test-ban treaty which the United States signed with Russia some weeks later seemed, to the French at least, to do just that.

The first six months of the year 1963 witnessed, as has been said, an unaccustomed lull in United States-Russian relations. The successful resolution of the Cuban crisis in the last months of the previous year doubtless contributed to it, but it more probably should be attributed to Soviet preoccupation with Communist China. Khrushchev's difficulties with Mao, it was widely agreed, were even more serious than Kennedy's differences with De Gaulle. The ideological and tactical conflict between Moscow and Peking had split Communist parties everywhere and had resulted in a strong challenge to Russia's leadership of the Communist world. The Chinese charged that the Russians had deserted the Marxist revolution by refusing to promote revolution in under-developed areas of the world, denounced Khrushchev's policy of "peaceful coexistence," and asserted that it was the primary job of the Communists to communize by force. The Russians answered that revolution was a dangerous game in the nuclear age, and asserted that the proper Communist strategy was to contain capitalism while encouraging the growth of Communist military and economic power. As this dispute grew more and more bitter, some experts on Russian affairs predicted that it would force Khrushchev to turn to the West. The test-ban treaty was perhaps a case in point.

Sometime in May, President Kennedy decided to attempt a dramatic infusion of life into the test-ban talks which had been stalled for a year or more. A commencement address at American University on June 10 provided him an opportunity to make a gesture of cooperation toward the Soviet Union. Kennedy knew, of course, that talks between China and Russia were to be held in Moscow at about the same time that Averell Harriman, Under Secretary of State for Political Affairs, was scheduled to go there to try again for a nuclear test ban. In his address the President denied that the United States sought to enforce a "Pax American" on the world by arms, and asked Americans to re-examine their attitude toward the Cold War; he declared that both the United States and the Soviet Union were "caught up in a vicious and dangerous cycle in which suspicion on one side breeds suspicion on the other, and new weapons beget counterweapons," and called on the Soviet Union to look westward for its natural allies against the rising belligerence of Communist China.

Khrushchev at first publicly sneered at the speech, but, whether because of an intensification of the Sino-Soviet quarrel or not, he soon agreed to negotiate. On July 2 in East Berlin, a few days after President Kennedy's tumultuous welcome on the other side of the Communist wall, Khrushchev declared his willingness to agree to a ban on nuclear tests provided it was linked with the signing of an East-West nonaggression pact. For the United States to have agreed to such a provision would have implied recognition of East Germany and thus its acceptance of a divided Germany. This it could not do without the approval of West Germany and France. After talks were safely under way, Khrushchev, fortunately for the success of the negotiations, agreed to drop the proviso.

On July 25, after ten days of discussion, the United States, the Soviet Union, and Great Britain concluded a treaty to prohibit nuclear testing in the atmosphere, in space and under water. It was the first treaty to come out of 18 years of negotiations on the arms race, and the only treaty since Austrian sovereignty was restored eight years ago to deal with a major issue of the Cold War. The treaty was of unlimited duration but it contained an abrogation clause that allowed each of its signatories to "withdraw from the treaty if it decides that extraordinary events related to the subject matter of this treaty have jeopardized the supreme interest of its country."

Even among those most likely to credit Russian good intentions, the mood was one of only cautious optimism. For one thing, the agreement left the signatories free to continue underground tests and it seemed certain that their military leaders, most of whom disapprove of any limitation on testing, would force them to do just that. For another, neither France nor China signed the treaty. In Paris, De Gaulle dismissed the test-ban agreement as irrelevant and called on France's Continental partners to stand together at a time when contacts were being renewed between the Russians and the Anglo-Saxons; in Peking, the Chinese denounced Premier Khrushchev's "open capitulation and open betrayal."

Despite its limitations, the treaty was an important milestone in East-West relations. In the first place, it promised to end pollution of the atmosphere by the United States and the Soviet Union. Secondly, it could bring a slowdown in the increase of atomic weapons, enough of which already exist to destroy the earth. Finally, it was surely important, after so many years of fruitless negotiation, to make a step—however short and hesitant—toward ultimate disarmament.

That the President would secure the two-thirds' vote in the Senate necessary for ratification of the treaty was never in doubt. But some influential Senators (among them Barry Goldwater who was already running for the Republican presidential nomination in 1964) opposed it, and many of those who announced their intention of voting for it were wary. During 12 days of hearings by the Senate Foreign Relations Committee, a number of important questions repeatedly were raised. Would the treaty prevent the United States from maintaining its nuclear superiority over the Soviet Union? Would it weaken the country against surprise attack? Would the United States continue testing underground? Underlying such questions was fear that any agreement with Russia was almost bound to be a trap. Such fears were partially assuaged by the testimony of the Secretaries of State and Defense, the Chairman of the Atomic Energy Commission, and the head of the Joint Chiefs of Staff, all of whom stressed the treaty's advantages for the United States. Finally on September 24, by a vote of 80 to 19, the Senate gave its approval.

Even before the United States ratified the treaty, Khrushchev had proclaimed a new era in United States-Russian relations, an era inaugurated by what he termed "the Spirit of Moscow," and by late September the Moscow press was speaking of the "favorable winds" that were blowing in international relations. The two countries took steps to conclude air-travel and consular agreements, and, more importantly, President Kennedy approved on October 9 the sale to the Soviet Union of 150,000,000 bushels of wheat for $250 million. There were several reasons for the wheat deal—the news that Canada was to sell $500 million worth of wheat to Russia, which unsettled the Middle West where America's own farm surpluses hang heavy; the fact that the sale of wheat abroad would reduce the burdensome surplus of about 1.2 billion bushels which costs the Federal government in storage and related costs almost $300 million annually; the possibility of redressing the U. S. balance of payments deficit, running at the rate of about $2.5 billion annually; and, finally, the desire of the Kennedy Administration to make the most of the relaxation of international tension.

Despite Khrushchev's occasional displays of truculence such as Russian harassments of American military convoys on the Autobahn to Berlin and the arrest of an American scholar in Moscow on espionage charges, the "Spirit of Moscow" continued to prevail during the fall and early winter. In the contrast between this atmosphere and the angry dispute between Russia and China perhaps lies a glimmer of hope that an understanding between East and West may at last be possible.

By the time the Senate acted on the test-ban treaty, the Administration and the public, taking ratification for granted, had transferred their attention to South Vietnam where a story of intrigue and adventure, assassination and conspiracy, was being enacted. For the United States the stakes were high; they were nothing less than the future of Southeast Asia.

The story of South Vietnam is one of gradual and increasing U. S. involvement in that country's bitter and bloody fight against communism. It began in 1954 when Vietnam, following the French disaster at Dien

Bien Phu, was partitioned at the Geneva Conference. The Americans counted on South Vietnam's Premier (later President), Ngo Dinh Diem, to keep his country a bulwark of anti-communism in Southeast Asia. Diem was hailed as one of the great statesmen of the new Asia, and was making considerable progress in land reform and economic development when Communist guerrillas from the north struck again in 1959. Soon after President Kennedy took office in 1961 it appeared that without American aid Diem's government might fall.

Vietnam was the second major Communist challenge the United States had had to face in the Orient since World War II. The first was in Korea where Peking and Moscow tested the willingness and ability of the United States to fulfill its world-wide commitment to freedom. The bloody and indecisive Korean War was our answer. The challenge of Vietnam was different but no less serious. Kennedy was well aware of the political pitfalls in the Vietnam situation. If U. S. aid were not given and the country went Communist, his opponents would be the first to campaign on the slogan "Who lost Southeast Asia?" For him to reply that the United States could not lose what it never had possessed would be, as he realized, futile. Anyway, the President was a firm believer in the "domino" theory—the theory that as Vietnam goes, so will go Laos, Cambodia, Burma, and perhaps even Thailand, Malaya, and Indonesia.

As the guerrillas (called Vietcong) won victory after victory, Kennedy intervened to prop up the Diem regime with money and soldiers. Beginning in late 1961, the U. S. operation in South Vietnam steadily expanded. By the summer of 1963 there were some 13,000 American military "advisers" in the country and American aid was totaling nearly $500 million a year.

Meanwhile, the defects of President Diem's regime were becoming increasingly obvious and more and more an obstacle to victory. Mistrustful of assistants outside of his family circle, Diem came to rely chiefly on his brother, Ngo Dinh Nhu, head of the secret police, and Nhu's masterful and volatile wife. As Diem himself became increasingly isolated and remote, the Nhus began to speak for his government. The strident and harsh tones which they used were no more to the liking of the United States than to the majority of the Vietnamese. For his part, Nhu sent tens of thousands of his political opponents to re-education camps or jails. For her part, Madame Nhu made herself the champion of Vietnam's women, banning concubinage and divorce. But she also prohibited gambling and dancing, thus alienating many fun-loving Vietnamese. Both of the Nhus, themselves Roman Catholics, advocated repressive measures against the Buddhists who constituted 70 percent of South Vietnam's population. The Buddhist protest against domination by a Catholic minority, as the Nhus well knew, was in large part an outlet and rallying cry for anti-Diem sentiment.

In May, 1963, police fired at rioting Buddhists, killing nine of them. For the next weeks, Buddhist protest marches were held in Saigon and other cities, ending in a horrific climax when a Buddhist priest burned himself to death. Through the summer, Buddhist demonstrations were stepped up and the government used increasingly brutal police tactics to repress them. Had it not been for the Vietcong guerrillas and the massive aid which it was giving Diem's government, the United States might have viewed Nhu's behavior as only one more example of domestic tyranny. But Vietnamese resistance to his policies was obviously impeding the war against the Communists. Early in August, President Kennedy appointed Henry Cabot Lodge, U. S. delegate to the United Nations during the Eisenhower Administration, Ambassador to South Vietnam. His mission was to safeguard American interests and to persuade Diem to concentrate on winning the war instead of stamping out Buddhist opposition to his government. Nhu's answer was given only a few days after Lodge arrived.

Shortly after midnight on August 20 hundreds of helmeted police, armed with shotguns, tear-gas grenades, submachine guns and carbines, poured through the gates of Saigon's main Buddhist temple. Hundreds of yellow-robed monks and nuns were herded into trucks and taken away. A few hours later, similar raids were made on dozens of pagodas throughout South Vietnam. All in all, some 1,000 monks were carted off to jail as were thousands of students who demonstrated against the government. The United States protested in the strongest criticism it had yet made of the Diem regime. On September 2 President Kennedy openly expressed doubt that Diem could win the war unless he changed his policies and the composition of his government. But the Nhus were not unduly disturbed by verbal brickbats; their concern was with continued American aid. Doubtless to their relief, the President announced a week later that the United States had no intention of suspending American aid to South Vietnam at present.

Nevertheless, the breach between Washington and Saigon was complete and lasting. By October the question was how long it would be possible for the two countries to collaborate effectively in military affairs. Nhu denounced Ambassador Lodge as "a man of no morals," and charged that the United States was "destroying my country's psychology." For its part, the Administration began to put the economic squeeze on Nhu and Diem by withholding financial aid. And whether or not Ambassador Lodge made the remark attributed to him by an American journalist that "the suspension of economic aid is by no means our trump card," the Kennedy Administration did not discourage efforts to overthrow the Diem regime.

On November 1, the *coup d'etat* took place. A military junta led by General Duong Van Minh ("Big Minh" to the Americans in Vietnam), a respected veteran of the war against the Communists, seized control. The take-over was quick and efficient. Diem's special forces who guarded the roads into Saigon were overwhelmed, key ministries and police centers were seized, and the cream-colored stucco palace of President Diem surrounded. Diem and Nhu escaped by an underground tunnel, but were captured in a suburban Catholic Church and killed. On Tuesday, November 5, the rebels installed a provisional government which included both civil and military figures. Real power, however, remained with the generals who had master-minded the revolt.

Washington's hopes that this junta would seize the initiative in the war against the Vietcong Communist guerrillas were quickly disappointed. The new government was initially so preoccupied with problems of consolidating its own rule that it paid too little attention to the war which was raging in the crucial Mekong River delta and, emboldened by the change of regime in Saigon, the Vietcong guerrillas took the offensive. In the month of November, a U. S. military report stated that the Communists launched more attacks and the South Vietnamese lost more weapons and territory than in any previous month of the year. By the end of the year 1963 there was gloomy talk in Washington about internal disorder in South Vietnam being endemic. Few U. S. officials believed that the South Vietnamese would rally wholeheartedly to the new government any more than they had to the old; few predicted that the generals who had seized control would exercise the leadership or make the sacrifices necessary to win what Secretary Dean Rusk called this "dirty, untidy, disagreeable" war.

Straightening out the tangled problems of South Vietnam was alone enough to tax the ingenuity of the State Department. But the Americans continued, as for the past decade and a half, to bear the burden of global problems. The Administration was busy trying to patch things up between Pakistan and India. It was placing little hope on Laos. It was trying to encourage President Sukarno of Indonesia into peaceful coexistence with a Malaysian federation. It was also betraying a preference for Colonel Nasser and a distaste for the Middle East's remaining kings and crumbling feudalism. It was attempting to build a dam of dollars to hold back the surging waters of discontent in Latin America.

On August 17, 1963, the Alliance for Progress, President Kennedy's inspiring dream of peaceful revolution in Latin America through U. S. aid, celebrated its second birthday. One's assessment of its accomplishments, obviously, depends on the yardstick by which he judges progress. It was nonetheless certain that, despite the support given it by Congress and the patient efforts of President Kennedy, it had fallen short of the goals so confidently set for it in 1961. President Kennedy himself said early in August: "We have a long, long way to go, and in fact in some ways the road seems longer than it was when the journey started."

Nevertheless, there were solid accomplishments of which the Alliance could boast. Ten Latin American countries had changed their income tax systems and seven had passed land reform laws. The effectiveness of these reforms, of course, would be determined by their implementation. More important, half-a-dozen countries had produced integrated schemes for economic and social development. In its first two years, furthermore, the United States had committed a total of over $2 billion to the Alliance and disbursed over $1.5 billion of it in the 1962 and 1963 fiscal years. The projects for which this money was spent included low-cost housing projects, roads, aid to industry, economic planning, and educational, medical, and social welfare assistance.

Given these achievements, why did the Alliance still have so poor a reputation? In Latin America there was widespread public disenchantment and listlessness toward the Alliance, considered either as an idea or as a program. In view of the long history of Latin American hostility toward any interference in its affairs by the United States, it was understandable that any U. S. program would be viewed suspiciously. To many Latins, U. S. exhortations to self-improvement and collective responsibility were considered as just so many more unwarranted directives from Washington. The United States, moreover, may have made a mistake in emphasizing the importance of the Alliance as a counter to Castroism. Such an emphasis allowed some Latin Americans, however unfairly, to argue that U. S. generosity was based on America's military and strategic self-interest. By the Alliance's second birthday it was obvious that the Cuban revolution was not going to be imitated by other Latin American countries;

Castro's most ardent admirers admitted that the Cuban revolution was an oddity and that no point would be served in trying to travel the same road. But the U. S. effort to promote the Alliance as part and parcel of anti-Cubanism and at the same time to stress its importance in bringing about internal social reform in Latin American countries left many Latins confused. Was socialism supposed to drive out socialism? How radical a government would the United States allow?

But the greatest drawback to the success of the Alliance was political instability. The Alliance was founded on the idea that economic and social progress must come about in the framework of freedom and political democracy. How could the United States insure democratic government in an area which had not yet truly broken with its colonial or feudal past? Edwin Martin, Assistant Secretary of State for Inter-American Affairs, pointed out the virtual impossibility of doing so. "Nor can we, as a practical matter, create effective democracy by keeping a man in office through the use of economic pressure or even military force when his own people are not willing to fight to defend him," he said. "A democracy dependent on outside physical support of this kind is a hollow shell which has no future." The problem, however difficult it may be to solve, became an acute one in 1963. Military upheavals in country after country, accompanied by what many Latin Americans regarded as U. S. approval of the upheavals, helped weaken the political and ideological standing of the Alliance.

During the year military coups in Latin America overturned four civilian governments. In April, the government of Guatemala was overthrown just on the eve of democratic elections; on July 11, a military coup ousted Ecuador's president; on September 25, U. S. hopes for democracy in the Dominican Republic crumbled when a military junta arrested Dr. Juan D. Bosch, the leader of a constitutional and democratic government, and seized control; eight days later, Honduras followed the lead of the Dominican Republic. The pattern of the military coup was similar in each case: the military either initiated the revolt or was the decisive factor in its outcome, the revolt was carried out in the name of anti-communism, and a military junta was in control of the government that emerged.

By the time Lyndon Johnson became President, it was clear that the lessons learned in the brief history of the Alliance for Progress required a re-evaluation of the techniques and procedures employed in managing it. Johnson, no more than Kennedy, could escape the reality of continued Latin American poverty, ignorance, and disease, and the problem of how to deal with them. Less than a month after taking office, Johnson set the stage for a drastic review of U. S. policy by naming Thomas C. Mann, the Ambassador to Mexico, to be director of all U. S. policies in Latin America. Declaring that "no work is more important for our generation of Americans than our work in this hemisphere," the President prepared to face the new Latin American realities.

How successfully Johnson would meet these and other challenges of the presidency remained, of course, to be seen. The presidential picture which emerged during the few weeks he occupied the White House in 1963 was of a political virtuoso intent on wooing all segments of American opinion, an able and astute party chieftain who might restore harmony to a bitterly divided Democratic party, and an Executive who would use his considerable parliamentary skill to cajole and coerce Congress into passing his legislative program.

From the day he acceded to the presidency, Johnson began looking for an opportunity to assert his influence over Congress. He first attempted to get the tax cut bill out of the Senate Finance Committee. When Senator Byrd proved intractable, he tried to persuade the House to adopt the civil rights bill before adjournment. The House would not act so quickly. Neither was it possible to salvage the drastic cut already made in foreign aid, a reduction of $1.5 billion from the Administration's original request. He did, by a show of determination and toughness, force Congress to drop an amendment to the foreign aid bill which would have prohibited the Export-Import Bank from guaranteeing private credits for the sale of wheat or any other commodity to Communist countries; he also had the satisfaction of signing a measure providing Federal aid to college construction which Congress passed in December. Other major items of the Kennedy program such as medicare and Federal aid to public elementary and secondary schools remained on the congressional calendar for 1964.

Reporters and experienced political analysts speculated a great deal on Johnson's parliamentary skill and concluded that he might be able to coerce a reluctant Congress into passing the legislation which President Kennedy had urged without success. Such a prediction might come true, but it overlooked several factors which might mitigate against it. In the first place, the fact that President Johnson is a Southerner does not mean that the Southerners who control so much of the machinery of Congress will follow his leadership. In the second place, the legislative wizardry which he displayed during his years as Senate majority leader might be of scant use to him as President. The techniques of persuasion and coercion which he employed while a Senator might arouse only resistance if employed by the Executive.

To relate United States history—whether of an era, a decade, or a single year—solely from the vantage point of the White House, the State Department, or the Congress is to slight much of the richness, variety, and complexity of American life. In a longer study, the scientific and technological changes that for a decade have been transforming society would be analyzed; the literature which often mirrors society, reflecting its mood and its values, would be described; the diversions by which people escape the routine of the factory, the drudgery of the office, or the cares of public office would be related. We cannot, however, neglect some of the lurid feature stories which highlight the darker side of American life.

The most publicized of the latter tales were told to congressional committees. The revelations made by Joseph Valachi were a shocking reminder of the power, wealth, and influence of crime in the United States; the story unearthed about Bobby Baker was a sad commentary on the ethical standards of some American businessmen and public servants.

Under television floodlights, Valachi told the Senate Investigating Committee spine-chilling stories of the New York underworld. As millions of TV watchers shuddered, he related gory stories of Cosa Nostra, the underworld crime syndicate which is also known as the Mafia or the Black Hand. In a rich Brooklyn accent he described the "kiss of death" by which informers such as himself are marked for extinction, and the initiation by blood and fire. Not since the Kefauver hearings twelve years ago had the public been treated to such a candid account of underworld intrigue and murder. Whatever the importance of Valachi's revelations (members of the New York police force, for example, derided them as "stale underworld gossip"), they did emphasize that racketeering continues to be big business in the United States, and that crime has become a way of life for large numbers of Americans.

The political scandal of the year was the Bobby Baker case. Baker had risen from the humble rank of a Senate page boy to the post of secretary to the Senate majority leader. It was revealed that while occupying the latter job at a salary of less than $20,000 a year Baker had accumulated a large fortune. Investigations unearthed a number of financial deals—contracts for placing vending machines in aircraft factories and space laboratories with government contracts, for example— in which Baker allegedly had used his influence as a behind-the-scenes power in the Senate to enrich himself. The investigation, with its hints of wild parties involving government personalities and German models, suggested more than it revealed, and it was not proved that Baker had violated any specific law. It did point up, however, the larger question of official ethics. Should officers and members of Congress be allowed to use their official positions to enrich themselves? Should they not be required by law to reveal all their sources of income? What should be done to curb the lobbyists with whom Baker allegedly had such a close and profitable relationship? In one sense, the Congress itself was on trial in the Baker case, but that the hearings would result in self-imposed reform appeared highly unlikely.

If the Valachi and Baker stories revealed the seamy side of American life, the record of the Peace Corps highlights the humanitarianism and idealism which still characterize it. In 1963 the Corps celebrated its second birthday and was, by general accord, an unqualified success. In Africa, for example, 1,500 volunteers—most of them between the ages of 21 and 25—were carrying on such programs as road surveys in Tanganyika, heavy construction work in Tunisia, medical technology in Togo, and school teaching throughout the continent. As in Africa, so too in other underdeveloped areas— the Peace Corps was providing urgently needed technical assistance and demonstrating that the American interest in the rest of the world is not dictated solely by military and strategic considerations.

16449